HOLLAND
AND BRITAIN

CHARLES WILSON

---

11 PLATES IN COLOUR
AND
74 ILLUSTRATIONS. IN
BLACK & WHITE

COLLINS · LONDON
14 ST. JAMES'S PLACE

PRODUCED BY
ADPRINT LIMITED LONDON

PRINTED IN GREAT BRITAIN BY
CLARKE & SHERWELL LTD NORTHAMPTON
ON MELLOTEX BOOK PAPER MADE BY
TULLIS RUSSELL & CO LTD MARKINCH SCOTLAND

PLATES IN COLOUR

BLACK AND WHITE ILLUSTRATIONS

NORTH SEA

WEST FRIESIAN ISLANDS

• Franeker

FRIESLAND

Texel

• Helder

NORTH HOLLAND

• Enkhuizen

Alkmaar •

ZUIDER SEA

• Volendam
• Marken

Bloemendaal •

HAARLEM •

• AMSTERDAM

• Muiden

• Naarden

Leyden •

UTRECHT

• UTRECHT

GEL

• THE HAGUE

• Delft

Lek

Lower Rhine

HOOK VAN HOLLAND •

Schiedam •

• ROTTERDAM

SOUTH HOLLAND

De Waal

Brielle •

Helvoetsluis •

Dordrecht •

• Loevestein

Maas

• HERTOGENBOSCH

Zierikzee •

NORTH BRABANT

• Breda

Veere •

MIDDELBURG •

Flushing •

ZEE LAND

LI

BUR

• Ostend

• BRUGES

• ANTWERP

Scheldt

• BRUSSELS

• MAA

LIEGE •

MAP OF
HOLLAND

Showing the chief places
mentioned in the text

RONINGEN

DRENTHE

ERIJSSEL

ND

Rhine

COLOGNE

Scale of Miles

0   10   20   30   40   50   60

Scale of Miles

0   100

5   1
4
3   2
6

MAP OF ENGLAND & HOLLAND
Showing their relative position and
the chief cross-Channel routes

1 LONDON — AMSTERDAM	4 HARWICH — THE HOOK
2 LONDON — ROTTERDAM	5 EDINBURGH — DORDRECHT
3 HARWICH — THE BRILL	6 DOVER — OSTEND

7 DOVER — CALAIS

ERASMUS VAN ROTTERDAM, c. 1466-1536
Oil painting by an unknown artist

"I know some Persons of good sense and even of Quality that have no clearer notion of 'em tho' they are next door to us, than they have of the Mandarins in China ; and what is worse, think themselves no more obliged to know the one than the other . . ."

BERNARD MANDEVILLE *Female Dialogues No 7*

INTRODUCTION

The Englishman has never shown much spontaneous enthusiasm for other people's history. Some more practical and immediate stimulus has usually been needed to persuade him that the history of foreigners can possibly be any concern of his. Sometimes the bait has been provided by current fashions in foreign policy. The Entente Cordiale generated a certain curiosity about the history of France : the addition of each new ally to the strength of the United Nations has provided the occasion for an ephemeral display of historical interest : the historian discovers a mission to tell the story of the American people : a passion for the history of Russia ceases to be the monopoly of members of the Left Book Club. At other times, the stimulus is provided by foreign travel, by the desire to know in advance (or more often in sentimental retrospect) about the castles of the Rhine, the ancient wealth of Bruges or the glories of Florence. Now in this kind of competition for the English reader's attention, the Netherlands were unfavourably placed. For more than two hundred years before the German invasion in 1940, the Dutch had been pledged to a neutral or at any rate static policy which, however sensible, afforded meagre opportunities for historical heroics in the grand manner: and indeed, on the day-to-day application of that policy, Englishmen and Dutchmen often found it difficult to see eye-to-eye. For Britain could dispense with the neutral's services better than could her enemies.

Even the heroic story of the national struggle which had appealed to the liberals of Motley's generation had less attraction for a generation which had learned by bitter experience that a nation which shapes its nationhood by the sword is too often apt to go on assuming that the sword is the normal instrument of policy in international affairs. Moreover, as anyone who crossed the Belgian or German border into Holland soon found to his cost, the pre-war rate of exchange was not calculated to encourage the Englishman to stay longer than was necessary to transact his business, spend quarter-of-an-hour at Marken or twenty minutes at Volendam, half a day round the Binnenhof or in the Bollenvelden by Haarlem : then he would leave Flushing or the Hook with a sigh—half of regret at leaving

NORTH VIEW OF LONDON
Pen and wash drawing by Michael Overbeck, c. 1620

so many good things unseen and uneaten, half of relief to be out of a country where bed and breakfast cost at least three or four times what he was accustomed to pay in France, Belgium or Germany, and where the only really cheap thing to be had was a cigar.

In the absence, then, of the twin aids of political fashion and cheap travel, the Englishman's interest in the history of Holland and its relations with his own country not unnaturally languished. It must be admitted that he did not get much help from the Dutchman, who brought modesty about his people's virtues and achievements nearer complete self-efface-ment than the English themselves. In Holland, as in England, a foreign label was a sure guarantee of success. And yet of all the foreign influences which have been brought to bear on English life, few have been more powerful, more profound or more lasting than that of the Dutch, who for the century and a half between 1600 and 1750, helped to shape not only our economic institutions, but our ideas on architecture, art, science, agri-culture, to say nothing of our conceptions of philosophy, theology and law. The origin of most of Britain's contacts with the Dutch during the most important period—say from 1600 to 1730—is to be found in the peculiarly close economic associations which grew up between the two countries during that period. Dutch sailors, shipwrights and merchants introduced many new words into our nautical vocabulary—words like yacht, sloop, boom, hoy, clinker, skipper—and a hundred others.

The student of Anglo-Dutch relations is naturally tempted to turn his attention to the period when the two countries were united under William of Orange or, even more effectively, under Marlborough and Heinsius ; but this was only the consummation of a long tradition of union, centuries when the economic interests of Britain and the Low Countries were com-plementary and not, as they later became, mutually exclusive. There is hardly a period in English history when ideas or people from the

THE YACHT HARBOUR, AMSTERDAM
Pen and wash drawing by Rembrandt van Rijn, 1606-1669

Low Countries have not influenced us in one way or another, and the earliest evidence of Flemish settlers in England goes far back into the Middle Ages, before the Norman Conquest. Later medieval times saw the growth of the English wool trade and the great cloth industry of Holland which looked to England and Scotland for its raw materials. From the wool trade came much of England's medieval wealth ; and as Governments saw the possibilities for good and ill, for peace and war, of a commerce which amassed large fortunes in the hands of small bodies of men, the wool trade ministered to the needs of British arms abroad, allied the King of England with Jacob van Arteveld, the rebel of Flanders, precipitating the struggle for power in the English Parliaments and dictating in part the balance of English society. In those days there were English merchants in Dordrecht, Middelburg and Bruges, and Flemish and Dutch merchants in the English seaports. But the relationship of the two regions was not wholly static. There was a slow, but continuous movement to deprive Holland of its industrial monopoly. Weavers from the Low Countries were granted Royal protection and economic privileges in London and other large cities, and at the close of the Middle Ages, England was in the position of an industrial competitor, toying from time to time with restrictions on the export of wool which were to become permanent in the later seventeenth century. It is, in fact, in the sixteenth, and especially in the seventeenth and eighteenth centuries that the Netherlands made their most notable contribution to English life—to art and letters as well as to our economic institutions and methods.

Trade and religious persecution brought close associations in the sixteenth century. Although English industries were now competing with the Dutch, the English took advantage of the strong Dutch mercantile interests and of internal municipal rivalries to keep a foothold in the Low Countries. Rotterdam, Delft and Middelburg competed for "mutual

13

friendship with the celebrated English nation" (in the shape of the Merchant Adventurers' Company) and not all the wrath of Amsterdam's industrial interests could ensure the expulsion of their rivals. Meanwhile England and Holland took it in turns to offer hospitality to each other's persecuted minorities. Hundreds of Dutch refugees from the Spanish terror found asylum in England. An address to Elizabeth presented by a number of the exiles ended with a tribute which has been echoed often enough in later years :

"For here is peace and quietnesse where as the moste parte of foraine countreys are full of great tumultes . . . We a numbre of us are arrived in saftie in this your Maiesties realme of Englande as unto a moste safe and sure harborough, where we live (God be thanked) under your Maiesties protection and safeguarde in great libertie to serve God in eyther language, the Frenche or the Dutche, without al feare of tyrantes."

The Puritan pilgrims who fled to Amsterdam and "the fair and beautifull citie" of Leyden a few years later would probably have found it difficult to share these sentiments. But as so often in English history, the foreigner apparently got more sympathy than the native, and the Dutch Church at Austin Friars witnessed a Protestant alliance between Dutch and Huguenot which lasted into the nineteenth century. There were other Dutch settlements at Norwich and Colchester, Rye, Canterbury and Southampton. The refugees were most numerous in the weaving industry, to which they brought a unique and specialised skill : in East Anglia they introduced the manufacture of new cloths. The Dutch weavers came over in considerable numbers between 1560 and 1570, settling down mostly at Colchester. Here the Dutch colony maintained its identity and its special privileges until 1728 when it finally died out. The history of the Dutch in this part of Essex is the history of the 'New Draperies,' for they it was who introduced bays, says, perpetuanas and bombazines, and as long as the trade flourished, so did the Dutch colony. Of course, there was friction, chiefly, it appears, with 'the meaner sort' of local inhabitants who were jealous of the aliens' wealth and talent: but, on the whole, they were respected as 'sober, honest and industrious' members of the community who brought wealth to the district and employment to the poor. The Government especially welcomed them, and an Act of Parliament confirming their privileges sets forth that the Dutchmen, by their honest dealing and industry had brought their trade of making bays, says, and other new draperies "into high credit, not only at home, but alsoe in fforraigne parts." Colchester bays, viewed and sealed by the Governors of the Dutch bay-hall, gave rise to a valuable export trade, chiefly to Spain and Portugal. Incidentally, the Dutch congregation at Colchester maintained close contacts with the congregation of the Church at Austin Friars. Not all the original immigrants settled down permanently in England ; some were only birds of passage who took back to Leyden and established there the peculiar forms of gild organisation which they found in East

GOLF ON THE ICE

Water colour drawing by Henrik Avercamp, 1585—c.1663

IN THE COURTYARD OF A DUTCH HOUSE
Oil painting by Pieter de Hooch, 1658

Anglia. But there were also Dutchmen in many other industries, in mining, in the metal and wire working industries, in drainage schemes. The Dutch technician was to the seventeenth century what the Scotch engineer was to the nineteenth century, but in even wider fields of economic activity. He was to be found wherever profitable occupation offered and he was in demand wherever Government or private enterprise was in need of technical or managerial skill.

According to Stow's *Annals*, the Dutch immigrants taught us many of the household arts, including that of starching. They also maintained a fund for supporting young Dutchmen at Cambridge and Oxford. Both Universities already had associations with one of the greatest Dutch scholars of all time, Erasmus of Rotterdam—Cambridge through Erasmus's friends Fisher and Cranmer, Oxford through Colet and More. Erasmus himself began his residence in Cambridge in 1510, bringing to the University Greek learning and scriptural criticism. His work bore fruit later. In 1548 it was ordained that Erasmus's paraphrases of the New Testament should be placed in every English church. Like his great successor Grotius nearly a century later, Erasmus insisted upon the reasonableness of religion. More than any of their contemporaries, these two great Dutch humanists anticipated the tolerance and even the rationalism of the eighteenth century. Ultimately, the English Protestant solution partook more of the flavour of Erasmus than of either Luther or Calvin.

In the seventeenth and eighteenth centuries, Dutch influences multiplied in number and power as the Golden Age unfolded across the North Sea. Artistic influences radiated from the Stuart Court, where from the time of Van Dyck, Mytens and Janssen onwards, Flemings and Dutchmen were accorded honours and commissions as Court painters. The galleries of hundreds of English country houses proudly showed their Lelys and Janssens and the Dutch masters introduced into English art a style of portraiture which held monopolys way into the eighteenth century. Perhaps the most formidable competitors for aristocratic favour were the Dutch marine painters like the younger and elder van de Veldes, both of whom were commissioned to work for the Court by the Charter of Charles II in 1675. Many of the best pictures of Jan van de Capelle found their way into English ownership in the eighteenth century, influencing Crome, Gainsborough and Constable ; while Albert Cuyp became the idol of the English collector.

The greatest of the English architects, Christopher Wren, came under the influence of contemporary Dutchmen like van Kampen. His assistant at Hampton Court, William Talman, the designer of Chatsworth and Dyrham Park, was a Dutchman ; so was Grinling Gibbons, who executed the interior woodwork for St. Paul's, many of Wren's City Churches, and Trinity Library. The increasing use of brick in building may be traced back to Dutch influence. English gardens were modelled on the Dutch pattern, with fountains, cisterns and lead statues and figures provided by craftsmen like the Dutchman John van Nost who kept a leadyard in Piccadilly and turned out a continuous stream of classical figures, cherubs and kneeling blackamores. The grandfather clock, with its inlaid woodwork and ornamented dial, was a Dutch fashion introduced by William of Orange, while his Queen brought with her the fashion for collecting Chinese porcelain—a fashion that was to reach its height in the positive mania for *chinoiserie* in the eighteenth century.

During this period, the Dutch reputation for industrial skill was further enhanced. In the shipbuilding and metal-working industries Dutch foremen and managers introduced the latest inventions and improvements. In the Midlands, the Black Country glass industry was founded and maintained by Flemish and Dutch capitalists. At Lambeth, Jan van Hamme obtained a patent in 1671 "for the art of makeinge tiles and porcelane and other earthenwares after the way practised in Holland." This was the beginning of the English Delft industry which spread later to Liverpool and Bristol. Some of the fashions originated at Lambeth (notably what we know as "Astbury ware") were probably inspired by the china figures and statuettes brought back from China by the Dutch East India merchants. Dutch fashions held their own until the second half of the eighteenth century when the flow was reversed and even the Dutch came to prefer the designs of Wedgwood to their native products.

The parts of England where the Dutch immigrants settled most thickly still display evidence of the wealth, energy and artistry of this remarkable community. In many parts of the Eastern Counties, but especially round Colchester and Norwich the stepped or scroll gable became almost a native style. Henry Bell's Custom House at Kings Lynn might well masquerade as the *Waaghuis* in any seventeenth century Dutch urban setting. Many East Anglian seventeenth century buildings are built of the typical small Dutch bricks which were shipped from Rotterdam and Amsterdam to Boston, Lynn, Yarmouth and Harwich either as cargo or ballast. Along with the bricks came the Delft tiles which were almost as popular in seventeenth century England as in Holland. At Norwich, the Old Meeting House had a pavement of Dutch bricks brought back by Puritan emigrants from Holland.

Further inland, in Cambridgeshire and the Holland parts of Lincolnshire, lay a land of fens, dykes, windmills and tulips strongly reminiscent

HARBOUR SCENE
Earthenware panel. Bristol, eighteenth century

16

HUNTING IN NORTHERN WATERS
Tile picture in enamelled earthenware by Cornelius Boermeester, c. 1700

of the other Holland over the water—a place where a Dutchman could feel at home. Here there is ample evidence of the work of another colony of Dutchmen who settled in the first half of the seventeenth century to help the Dutch engineer Cornelius Vermuyden to drain the Fens. The Dutch drainage workers had churches of their own at Thorney, and further north at Sandtoft, while at Ramsey some of the streets, for instance Le Munner-straate, still have Dutch names. At Fen Stanton, north of Cambridge, the cottages by the Church still show their mounting gables, while a mile or two across the meadows at Fen Drayton there are other Dutch houses including the one where (as local legend has it) Vermuyden himself lived. And over the door, carved in bold letters in the stone is the motto in Dutch —*Niet Zonder Arbeit* (Not without Labour).

Down in the west, the merchants and seafaring people of Devon had close and long associations with the Netherlands. From the sixteenth century, the merchants of Exeter had found their best market for Devonshire cloth in Amsterdam : in return they had bought Haarlem linens, and sail cloth for British ships. The great port for this trade was Topsham on the Exe. Topsham's days as a great port came to an end in the eighteenth century, but its deserted wharves and its handful of Dutch gabled houses are a reminder of days when great Devonshire merchants like Sir John Elwill spoke Dutch, when Amsterdam Captains could be seen in the streets of Exeter, and names like Steenwyke, van der Bush and Hochmeester were well-known from Tiverton to Exmouth. A few of the names (like Verhoeven) still survive in these parts.

17

London has always had her colony of Dutch merchants and artists (the Old Palace at Kew and the nearby cottage also in the Dutch style were originally built for a Dutch merchant) and from about 1650 onwards it grew in numbers and wealth. The centre of the colony always remained the Church in Austin Friars, now unhappily totally destroyed by German bombs. Only a few of the memorial stones to the leaders of the colony remain. They are mostly the names of merchants and financiers who had come over to manage the investment of Dutch money in the English National Debt in the eighteenth century ; for between 1710 and 1780 every class of Dutch investor owned shares in the Bank of England, the East India Company, the Assurance Companies or in consols or annuities. Many of these merchants and bankers upon whom the Treasury relied for assistance— Muilman, de Neufville, van Notten, de Smeth, Crayesteyn, Backers, Willink—were members of the Church. Some, like Jan van Hemert and Christian Woesthoven, were Deacons. Charles van Notten and his son were both elders : but the leaders of the colony were undoubtedly Gerard and Joshua van Neck, the sons of the Paymaster of William III's land forces. For his services to the Government (he was attached to the Walpole interest and later to the Duke of Newcastle) Joshua was granted first a baronetcy and later an Irish Peerage. Another influential member of the colony was the financier Gilbert de Flines, a descendant of Joost van den Vondel, the great Dutch poet and contemporary of Milton. Long after the original Dutch supporters of the Revolution—the Albemarles, the Portlands and Athlones—had become indistinguishable behind their English titles, this mercantile community retained its Dutch characteristics and connections and maintained a real corporate existence which centred round the Dutch Church (itself conveniently near the Bank of England and Change Alley). This was the Christian community but there were also many Sephardic Jews from Holland, who in 1700 built themselves a copy of their Amsterdam synagogue in Bevis Marks which has fortunately survived the raids.

By 1740 or 1750 it was all over : England could only borrow money where once she had sought inspiration. It was inevitable that in a world where power was to be measured in terms of coal, iron and steel, the Dutch should decline in importance : but the decline was hastened by the inability of her governing class to face the realities of a changing economic and political situation. During the period we rightly call the Golden Age of Holland, a period so astonishingly fertile in ideas and innovations that it seems to combine the features of an artistic and intellectual Renaissance with a miniature industrial and scientific Revolution, England had learned much from her Dutch neighbours. Had these contributions any particular qualities by which they could be distinguished? Is there any homogeneity to link the ideas of Erasmus or Grotius with the discoveries of Huygens or Boerhaave, to link the painting of Terborch with the charts of Lucas Wagenaer ? I think there is. There are certain inherent qualities in the

Dutch way of life and thought : these qualities in turn have something in common. In scientific matters, it showed itself as a love of precision and a determination to root out inaccuracy and superstition ; in economic affairs, it became a flair for making the best of what comes to hand, for making bricks without straw ; in social questions it was a passion for orderliness and cleanliness ; artistically, it was a passion for detail, for illuminating the homely subject by accurate observation, a peculiar fitness of means to ends ; intellectually, it was a profound belief in reasonableness; negatively, the avoidance of all flamboyance and exaggeration.

These are what the south is apt to regard as northern qualities, what the supercilious will write off as bougeois virtues, what at best distills into pure wisdom, and at worst may degenerate into dull unimaginativeness and mere money-grubbing. For good or for ill, this was the character of the Dutch genius which helped to transform England from a feudal into a modern society. "Saxon, or Norman, or Dane are we" sang the poet ; had space permitted he might have added that we are also Dutch, for a great deal that was Dutch became bonded into the English fabric in these years.

SYNDICS OF THE ST. LUKE'S GUILD OF HAARLEM
Oil painting by Jan de Bray, 1675

HOLLAND: BRITAIN'S SCHOOL OF TRADE

It is scarcely an exaggeration to say that in 1600, the United Provinces were the only major Power in Europe which conducted trade and finance on truly commercial principles, which did not in fact, subordinate economic policy more or less arbitrarily to politics and war. Of course, the system was not perfect: municipal and provincial rivalries were bitter and sometimes proved a considerable obstacle to trade, but what was important was that the laws which governed trade were made by merchants for merchants and were not permanently subject to the overriding authority of a government whose main preoccupations were military or dynastic and the raising of money to carry out their plans. Dutch policy was, therefore, the envy of merchants in these other less fortunate countries, amongst which was Britain. Meanwhile, the diligence, ingenuity and wealth of the Dutch had become proverbial. A glance at the central commercial institution of the United Provinces—the Amsterdam Bourse—will show something of the nature and scope of this world-wide economy. Unhappily, the old Bourse, built by Hendrik de Keyser in 1609, was burnt down more than a century ago, but many prints and plans have survived. To English eyes, the Bourse looks rather like a mixture of the Courts of two of the Cambridge Colleges—Neville's Court, Trinity, and First Court, Emmanuel. If you can imagine that each of the many pillars round Neville's Court represents the meeting-place of a particular group of merchants— the Russia merchants congregating round one, the Levant traders round the next, the East India merchants round a third, and so on, while in the open Court the brokers and financiers haggle over the day's share-quotations—you will have some idea how the system worked. The Bourse was, in fact, the hub of a gigantic network of world trade, shipping and

NEVILLE'S COURT, TRINITY COLLEGE, CAMBRIDGE
Engraving by David Loggan from his *Cantabrigia Illustrata*, 1690

THE COURT OF THE AMSTERDAM BOURSE
Engraving by Michael Colyn, 1609

finance. That economy was served by a vast fleet of merchant shipping. It is not possible accurately to estimate the tonnage employed, but even at the end of the century, when British competition was becoming serious, it was calculated that the Dutch still had roughly twice as much merchant shipping as the British, and almost ten times as much as the French. The Amsterdammer of those days might well have echoed the words of Pericles in the Funeral Speech : "Because of the greatness of our city the fruits of the whole earth flow in upon us : so that we enjoy the goods of other countries as freely as of our own." For Amsterdam was, like ancient Athens, an *emporion,* and like all *emporia* through the centuries—like Athens, Alexandria, Marseilles, Venice, Genoa, Antwerp and London— Amsterdam was full of strange people whose doctrines and ideas were at least as varied as their merchandize and their currencies. Andrew Marvell wrote (not in any spirit of admiration):

"Hence Amsterdam, Turk, Christian, Pagan, Jew,
Staple of sects and mint of schisme grew :
That bank of conscience, where not one so strange
Opinion but finds credit and exchange."

It is impossible to appreciate the strong influences which the Dutch exerted upon England in the seventeenth century unless it is first realised how fast this country was caught in the net of international trade which centred round Amsterdam. Amsterdam was for a period the market to which British goods were sent for sale and the *entrepôt* where British retailers bought the goods needed for the home market. It was also the currency and banking centre, the repository of economic experience and commercial intelligence, the one place in Europe where a buyer could always be put into contact with a seller or *vice-versa*. A long and arduous struggle was necessary before London was able to oust it from this commanding position. During the early stages of the process, the efforts of British merchants and pamphleteers amounted to little more than attempts to analyse the sources of Dutch prosperity and to urge the importance of imitating Dutch methods.

During the first three quarters of the seventeenth century, England was pre-occupied with internal political troubles and it was not until the last decades of the century that English writers began to catalogue for praise and imitation those virtues of the Dutch commercial system which had long been the object of English envy. A mass of booklets, pamphlets, and translations on Holland flooded the presses. From them, we may select three authors whose writings did more than anything else to shape the average Englishman's ideas about the Dutch in the seventeenth and eighteenth centuries—Sir William Temple, Sir Josiah Child and the Anglicized Dutchman, Bernard Mandeville.

Child's *Brief Observations concerning Trade and the interest of Money* was written during an enforced leisure in 1665, the year when the Plague raged in the City. Child's work has been called "almost the parent of our modern science of political economy," and it engendered bitter controversies which lasted thirty years. Here is the merchant *pur sang* jealously eyeing, across the North Sea, the mercantile paradise of his rivals for the East India trade. "The prodigious increase of the Netherlands" writes Child "in their domestic and foreign trade, riches and multitude of shipping, is the envy of the present, and may be the wonder of all future generations : and yet the means whereby they have thus advanced themselves are sufficiently obvious, and in a great measure imitable by most other nations, but more easily by us of this Kingdom of England." The recipe was a mixture of fifteen ingredients of which the following were the most important : the Dutch traded honestly, and methodically : they wisely taught their children arithmetic and book-keeping in the schools : they encouraged inventions and new manufactures : they had set up banks : they had introduced laws under which trade disputes were quickly settled and bills for debts were transferable from one man to another : "their councils of state and war include trading merchants that have lived abroad in most parts of the world, who have not only the theoretical knowledge but the practical experience of trade, by whom laws and orders are contrived and plans projected, to the great advantage of their trade." (This point recurs almost as frequently in seventeenth century writers as similar criticisms of the Civil Service do in the Press to-day.) Most

CHARLES II VISITS THE ESTATES OF HOLLAND
Drawn by F. J. Vliet and engraved by T. Matham, 1660

miraculous of all, however, they had succeeded in reducing their rate of interest to three per cent. (as against six per cent. in England). "This," says Child, "in my poor opinion is the *causa causans* of all the other causes of riches in that people : and if interest of money were with us reduced to the same rate as it is with them, it would in a short time render us as rich and as considerable in trade as they now are." As to how this seventeenth century social credit scheme was to be achieved, however, he is understandably less clear. As Child himself realised, the low rate in Holland was the result of a series of inter-acting financial mechanisms, which enabled wealth to be transferred from man to man. But we were only just beginning to learn and our economy was still stiff and inflexible.

A few years later, in 1673, Temple published his *Observations on the United Provinces of the Netherlands* which became a best-seller immediately and long remained the standard authority on the Netherlands. It is a broader, more gracious survey than Child's, touching upon most aspects of Dutch life and history. Nevertheless, the section on Dutch trade has much in common with Child's. Temple attributes Dutch prosperity to their "industry and parsimony" (a point which, as we shall see later, provoked Mandeville to contradict and dispute) ; like Child, Temple was also struck by the low rate of interest which prevailed, causing "so much money to lye ready for all Projects, by which gain may be expected . . ." Then there were the Banks, the Dutch system of justice, the convoy system which reduced their shipping losses, the "lowness of customs and freedom of ports," their orderly methods of conducting business, which was managed by men bred and born to trade ; the profitable fishing industry and the even more profitable colonial trade. His final verdict is very much like Child's. Dutch success, says Temple, is not the result of mere accident, "but of a great concurrence of Circumstances, a long course of Time, force of Orders and Method, which never before met in the World to such a degree, or with so prodigious a Success, and perhaps never will again."

The third of our authors, Bernard Mandeville, writing partly to correct some of Temple's errors and flatly denying some of the principles which Temple held in common with many contemporary writers on political economy, is the most stimulating and disconcerting of the three. He was a Dutchman, born at Dordrecht and trained as a doctor in the Medical School at Leyden. Coming to London, he set up a medical practice, though apparently without conspicuous success, for tradition has it that he was compelled to eke out his income by writing for the distillers "in defence of spirituous liquors." Certainly this would accord with his economic principles, which are indicated in the title of his best known work *The Fable of the Bees, or Private Vices Public Benefits*. Just as virtue is based on purely selfish interests, says Mandeville, so property is based on private vice or luxury and is increased by expenditure and not (as Temple had argued) by thrift or parsimony. Temple's prophecies about the Dutch decline had not been fulfilled : Holland was still a land of luxury and, therefore, according to Mandeville, of prosperity. Mandeville's philosophy had a good deal of influence later in the century. Dr. Johnson, for example, was strongly impressed by Mandeville's arguments and always vigorously defended luxury as a source of employment and distributor of wealth.

So much for the writers who drew England's gaze to the achievements of the Dutch. But already much more intimate connections were being formed. The Revolution of 1688 turned Child's exhortation into a prophecy and inaugurated a period of direct imitation of Dutch institutions. William himself arrived backed by Dutch guilders : a few years later, Britain found herself with a Funded National Debt on the Dutch model, and a Bank of England set up with capital assistance from Amsterdam. All this did not go unopposed. The Bank was a Whig Bank, supplying a Whig Government with money for a Whig war. Small wonder that the Tory country gentlemen, looking on in helpless frustration, bitterly dubbed the system "Dutch Finance." But mixed with their Jacobite xenophobia was a strong element of economic truth. The system of Government finance which was forged to arm, victual and maintain Marlborough's armies on the European Continent (and which in spite of Cobbett has survived substantially down to the present day) was moulded on the Dutch pattern, and in the process not a few Dutch hands were employed. Now

THE DUTCH CHURCH OF AUSTIN FRIARS, LONDON
Water colour by George Shepherd, fl. 1800-1830

we begin to encounter the names of some of the famous Portuguese
Jewish families who had taken refuge in Holland a century earlier—the
Medinas, the de Suassos and de Pintos—as well as Dutch Christian names
which were to be well-known in Change Alley and Jonathan's Coffee
House for a hundred years—the van Necks, van Nottens, van Hemerts
and many others. Their function was to supply, or at least procure and
pay for, the waggon loads of bread and cartloads of ammunition required
for the great military campaigns which Britain's armies were waging from
the Low Countries to the Danube. And in course of time, they crossed
the threshold, not merely of Jonathan's Coffee House but of Lloyd's,
the British Treasury, the Gentleman's Magazine and—final triumph—
the House of Lords.

At the same time, the lawyers, attorneys and brokers were busy devising processes and drawing up documents whereby Dutch investors
were enabled to put their spare funds into British Government shares
and annuities. For British Government finance had already begun to have
a reputation for safety and security : indeed, French writers often attributed British military success to our superior credit in Europe and
especially in Holland. The British Funds were quoted regularly on
the Amsterdam Bourse : not even the South Sea Bubble could shake
the British reputation for fair dealing. Dutch merchants, magistrates,

patricians, widows, orphans and Admirals, in fact Netherlanders of every class and profession, invested in British Government securities. The Bank of England had considerable numbers of Dutch shareholders until well into the nineteenth century.

Straightforward investment was accompanied by more daring speculation, based on intelligence (the word must cover everything from advance tips from those in the know at His Majesty's Treasury to gossip manufactured quite unscrupulously in the coffee houses of Change Alley or the Kalverstraat) exchanged between London and Amsterdam. London's Dutch community, clustering round the Dutch Church at Austin Friars and the Synagogue at Bevis Marks in the heart of the City received bulletins from the Amsterdam Bourse two or three times a week *via* the packet boats which plied between Harwich and Helvoetsluys, and in return gave Amsterdam the latest news of the French war which was always either in progress or about to begin, or of the Duke of Cumberland's campaign against the rebels of the North, and the effect of these things on the affairs of the Bank, the East India Company or the Insurance Companies. In Change Alley, there grew up a system of investment and

THE ENGLISH CHURCH, AMSTERDAM
Engraving, 1693

26

THE SYNAGOGUE, AMSTERDAM
Engraving, 1693

speculation which so closely resembles that which the Amsterdam Bourse had known since the sixteenth century that it is impossible to doubt that the former was largely modelled on the latter. Here was all the financial apparatus which had been perfected at Amsterdam a hundred years earlier —continuations, backwardations, a contango day, puts and calls— in fact the whole intricate apparatus of the modern Stock Exchange. As war followed war, enormous loans were floated and in accordance with the eighteenth century system, the Dutch agents in London—the van Necks in particular—undertook to be responsible for raising capital, running into many millions of pounds, from Dutch investors. Two devices for raising money for the Government were always connected in the popular mind with the Dutch. One—lotteries with prizes in the shape of annuities—was immensely popular and was much used by the Government between 1709 and 1824, when it finally fell a victim to the increasing respectability of government. The other, the Excise (the word is derived from the Dutch 'accijns') though as much detested as the Lottery was approved, has survived. Originally borrowed from the Dutch model during the Commonwealth period, no subsequent government ever quite plucked up courage to abolish it, and as the National Debt grew inexorably during the eighteenth century, the Excise proved an indispensable source of revenue to meet the interest payments.

Whatever aspects of British commerce or finance we examine between 1650 and 1780, we find Dutch influence—in the new techniques of banking, currency and insurance (the first Chairman of Lloyd's was a Dutchman), in methods of taxation, in the technique of internal and external lending and speculation and in the general stock of economic ideas. On every side Dutch ideas were helping to shape British economic policy. To set out our debt to them shortly, we may say that they helped to transform Britain from a largely agricultural country into a modern commercial state : by means of the financial devices which Britain borrowed from the Netherlands, wealth was made more fluid and men were enabled to borrow and to lend, to invest and to speculate : under Dutch guidance, British merchants learnt the infinite possibilities of debit and credit. Even Adam Smith, writing a hundred years after Child, remained as fascinated as Child had been by the Dutch banking system of those earlier years. One of the most interesting digressions in the *Wealth of Nations* is the description of the Bank of Amsterdam. The theory sometimes mooted that Adam Smith owed his free trade theory to the writings of Sir Matthew Decker, a Dutch merchant settled in England and a man much at home with the Duke of Newcastle and the Treasury, is probably extravagant. It is nevertheless true that in surveying world commerce to find proof for his economic principles, Adam Smith could hardly have failed to be impressed by the working example of Holland, which came as near to a free trade economy as the eighteenth century could hope to come.

A study of pamphlets and Parliamentary debates of the eighteenth century show not only merchants but landed gentry and peers of the realm devoting much time to discussions of economic issues. Parliament argued about the National Debt, the Sinking Fund, bounties, duties, taxes, excise, with as much vehemence as they discussed political principles. Profit rather than glory was the theme of the eighteenth century ; a tune learned partly in Amsterdam, though the harmony came to be peculiarly English.

By Adam Smith's day, the Dutch hegemony had been shattered by the impact of Franco-British power politics. Commercial Holland was over-shadowed by the new industrial giants of Europe. By the nineteenth century, Dutch trade and finance had been dwarfed by these warlike rivals, and the Dutch economy was only slowly and painfully adjusted to changed conditions. Even in Dickens's London, however, traces and traditions of the former wealth of the Dutch colony remained. Readers of Dickens's *Christmas Carol* will recall how Scrooge sat and shivered with his gruel over a fire place "built by some Dutch merchant long ago, and paved all round with quaint Dutch tiles designed to illustrate the Scriptures." Possibly Dickens was drawing upon real life for his fantasy ; possibly Scrooge's house had once been the home of the van Hemerts or the eighteenth century Dutch miser Crayesteyn, for Charles Dickens knew

JACOB JACOBSZ TRIP, BURGOMASTER OF DORDRECHT
Oil painting by Rembrandt van Rijn, c. 1661

the City and its history as few have done; perhaps somewhere up by
Austin Friars or New Broad Street, Scrooge's Delft tiles may still display
their "Cains and Abels, Pharaoh's daughters, Queens of Sheba, Angelic
messengers descending through the air on clouds like feather beds,
Abrahams, Belshazzars, Apostles putting off to sea in butter-boats . . ."

CHARTS AND MAPS

The first necessity for the merchant venturing into overseas trade is a ship. For a little time—while he is content to navigate local waters with the help of local knowledge of tides, currents and coasts—he may need little more. But it will not be long before he is emboldened to go further afield : then he will call in the aid of the geographers and cartographers to supply him with aids to navigation.

The history of cartography in the sixteenth and seventeenth centuries is closely associated with a number of contemporary events—the geographical discoveries of the Portuguese, the Dutch and the British, the growth of sea-borne trade—especially Dutch trade—the scientific enquiries set on foot by the requirements of the navigators, and the development of printing and engraving which reached a high degree of excellence in both the Southern and Northern Netherlands. No other people could rival the Dutch in their achievements in all these fields, so that it is not surprising to find that cartography received its first great development in Amsterdam : practically all the maps published in the sixteenth and the first half of the seventeenth century can be attributed to the school of cartographers which first grew up in Holland in the sixteenth century.

The first two great map-makers of this period were both Flemings—Gerhard Kremer (better known as Mercator) 1512-1594, and his friend Abraham Ortelius (1527-1598). Their greatest work dates from the time before Spanish ambitions had driven a wedge into the homogeneous civilization of the Low Countries : historically and economically, their work is a legacy of the great days of Antwerp as the main *entrepôt* of Western Europe. Mercator and Ortelius were an ideal combination of academic and practical ability : Mercator was a mathematician by training: Ortelius a merchant who was attracted by his friend's work to the scientific study of geography : together, they helped to free geography from the tyranny of Ptolemy and the fantastic traditions of medieval legend and inaccuracy. Mercator's greatest work was his map of the world, as then known, on the projection principle with parallels and meridians at right angles : Ortelius's, the *Theatrum Orbis Terrarum*. Already the custom of having English maps engraved in Holland was beginning : Mercator engraved Camden's map of the British Isles in 1564. And the works of both were printed by Christopher Plantin and by Raphaelingen of Leyden. Already the way was paved for a school of scientific map makers, collaborating with a school of engravers capable of work of the necessary clarity and precision. But so far cartography was still groping for general principles : it was the work of the next generation of cartographers of the Northern provinces to apply themselves to the solution of the problems of the navigators and to the production of—amongst other works—the county maps of England. Of the two, the makers of the hydrographic charts—especially Wagenaer and Blaeu—are the more important : it is impossible to over-estimate their value to the seafaring community of Western Europe in the seventeenth century.

Lucas Janzoon Wagenaer of Enkhuizen on the Zuiderzee, unlike Mercator, seems to have started his career as a pilot on a cargo ship trading from his native port. Coasting perilously round the shores of Western Europe, he no doubt became only too conscious of the discrepancies and imperfections of the "books of the ports" on which pilots then had to rely. These note books merely gave the pilot the rough distance between one port of call and the next, the course he should try to steer, with possibly some scrappy information about the tides. In 1584, Wagenaer produced the first part of his *Spieghel der Zeevart van de Navigatie der Westersche Zee*. This was a collection of charts of the coasts of Europe between the Zuiderzee and Cadiz, engraved on copper plates and printed at Leyden by Christopher Plantin. The following year, the second part followed, containing charts of the coasts of the North Sea and the Baltic. In 1592, came the *Thresoor der Zeevaert* covering the coasts of Northern Ireland,

Cives Angliæ

Scotiæ Cives

Cives Hiberniæ

DETAIL FROM
Mercator's *Atlas*
1623

Scotland and the Arctic. Finally in 1598, appeared the *Enchuyser Zeecaertboek*. Wagenaer's works represented an extraordinary advance in the nautical literature and cartography of Europe: while they were not free from error, they were relatively orderly and accurate and such mistakes as appeared were later corrected by his followers. Besides the charts, they contained an introduction on navigation, a kind of rough nautical almanac and sailing directions. Except for Mercator's engravings, Wagenaer's works contained the first examples in which charts were engraved on copper plates.

They met with immediate success, and nowhere were they more welcome than in England. The first Latin edition of Part I of the *Spieghel* was dedicated to Queen Elizabeth, while the *Thresoor* contained summaries of the voyages of Drake and Cavendish. Lord Charles Howard of Effingham, Lord Admiral of England, quickly drew the attention of the Privy Council to the *Spieghel* as being an aid "very necessary to our seamen," and Anthony Ashley, Clerk to the Council, was instructed to translate it. The translation appeared at London in 1588 under the title *The Mariner's Mirrour* and became a standard work in England in the seventeenth and eighteenth centuries : so much so that it was responsible for a new term in hydrography—marine charts became known, by a debasing of the author's name, as "waggoners." Throughout the eighteenth century, we find "Newest Waggoners" being advertised. In France, by an even stranger extension of the same process, they were known as "chartiers."

Wagenaer's charts were reprinted and improved in many respects by another great Dutch cartographer, William Janzoon Blaeu, in his *Licht der Zeevaert* which in 1617 was translated into English with the title *The Light of Navigation*. It would be no exaggeration to say that every seaman, British or Dutch, who sailed between Spitzbergen and the Canaries in the seventeenth and eighteenth centuries, used the charts of Wagenaer or one of his pupils.

Wagenaer's value was not overlooked by the Dutch authorities, who in their official encouragement of cartographers and inventors of navigational devices anticipated the British Government by more than a century. In 1585 he was granted a pension by the States of Holland : further awards from the same authorities and from the States General followed in 1598. In the same year, we find Wagenaer sitting on a committee with Scaliger, the philologist, Stevin, Snellius and van Collen (all mathematicians) to enquire into the claims of Plancius and Syvertzoon to have devised a process for working out longitude at sea—a problem which puzzled and to the end defeated the seventeenth century. It is perhaps worth mentioning that the first man definitely known to have made a marine time-keeper specifically designed to find longitude at sea was Christiaan Huygens, the Dutch scientist who ranks with Leibnitz and Newton in the versatility of his genius. Unfortunately, Huygen's time-keeper was not provided with compensating mechanism, and the solution

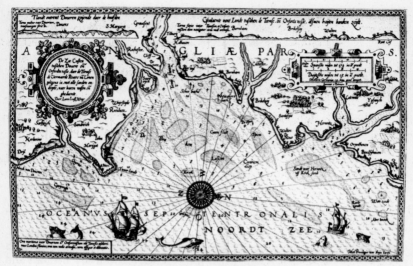

MAP OF THE THAMES ESTUARY
Engraving from Wagenaer's *Atlas*, 1588

of the problem had to await the appearance of Harrison's chronometer almost a century later. Nevertheless, the incident shows how sailors, scientists and engravers, collaborated with the authorities in seventeenth century Holland to solve the problems of trade and navigation.

Close as was the connection of the Dutch hydrographers with England (Huygens himself was a Fellow of the Royal Society) it was followed by even more intimate association in the persons of the two Hondiuses, the Janssens and the Blaeus, who mapped the English counties. The curious alliance of English and Dutch skill seems to have begun with two early Dutch engravers, Peter van der Keere and Jacob van Langeren, who engraved the maps of English counties by Christopher Saxton, John Speed and William Camden, in the late sixteenth and early seventeenth centuries. The works of these three map-makers also formed the basis of the maps by later Dutch cartographers. Jan Janssen's map of Cambridgeshire of 1646, for example, was based on an earlier one by Speed, bordered with beautiful and elaborate shields containing the arms of the Cambridge colleges. It was printed by Janssen at Amsterdam. Later reprints appeared, one of the best being the 1688 reprint by Gerard Valk and Peter Schenk. Janssen's great rival Johan Blaeu included in his four volume work the *Theatrum Orbis Terrarum* (1638) maps of the English counties, with the text of Camden's *Britannia* in Latin. Blaeu's volumes were also reproduced many times later in the century. Henry Hondius, of Amsterdam, also produced a number of sectional maps of Great Britain, including the first engraved map of the Great Level of the Fens in 1632. Whether

33

Hondius had any special connection with the fen drainage schemes undertaken by the Dutch engineer Vermuyden, it is difficult to say. At any rate his map is dedicated to the Duke of Bedford "and the other adventurers." It covers the area between Cambridge in the South, Peterborough in the West, Boston in the North and Brandon in the East. Ten years later, Vermuyden himself produced a map of exactly the same area, no doubt based on Hondius's, to illustrate his *Discourse touching the Drayning the Great Fennes* . . . Six years later, in 1648, Johan Blaeu followed with another map, no doubt carefully copied from the two previously described but distinguishable by having the title set in the right-hand bottom corner in a rectangular panel, supported by an abundance of fruits, and agricultural implements. Some time before this Hondius and Blaeu had gone into partnership at Amsterdam : evidently they were already well-known in England, as John Evelyn made a point of visiting their shop during his visit to Holland in 1641, buying maps and folios.

The great period of map-making in the Northern Netherlands lasted a little more than a century : it was overtaken by the growth of the French school, founded about the middle of the seventeenth century by Sanson of Abbeville, who started by copying the works of the Dutch cartographers. Nevertheless, the tradition of the Amsterdam engravers lived on. In 1700, Valk and Schenk, whom we have encountered selling the maps of Janssen, issued a complete set of county maps of England, Wales and Scotland. English map-makers still went to Amsterdam to have their maps engraved : we hear of Sir William Petty (who probably caught his enthusiasm for map-making while he was a student at Leyden) having his great map of Ireland "engraved at Amsterdam for £1,000."

The cartographers of the great period of the art in Holland took the whole world for their province : they mapped, with varying degrees of accuracy, not only the countries of Europe, but the continents of Africa, Asia and North and South America as well. The purpose of this survey is to indicate the importance of their work in mapping the coasts of Britain and the broad acres of the English shires, a task which produced some of their most remarkable and beautiful engravings.

The contribution of the Janssens, Hondiuses and Blaeus was not as indispensable as that of Wagenaer, nor was their work as original as the work of the earlier English map-makers upon whose maps they usually relied—John Speed, Christopher Saxton and Camden. But by adding the art of engraving to that of cartography, they made the geography of the British Isles known not only to Englishmen but to Europeans everywhere. Through the hundreds of maps which issued from the presses of Leyden and Amsterdam, men attained a reliable knowledge of the English towns and countryside where previously they had relied on travellers' tales or the equally imaginative maps of the Middle Ages. That these Dutch maps of England belong to a period when Britain had three major wars against the Dutch only makes them more remarkable.

THE HARBOUR, AMSTERDAM
Engraving c. 1600

HARWICH TO THE HOOK 1600—1800

For the seventeenth century Londoner, it was easier to travel from England to Holland than it was to visit Lincolnshire or Cornwall : even in 1700 it was easier for a London merchant to send a letter to a correspondent in Amsterdam than to a customer in Hull. Easy communications help to explain the continual flow of travellers which took place between Britain and the Netherlands—the ambassadors, politicians, soldiers, students, tourists, artists, merchants and spies who swelled the passenger lists of every ship that sailed from Harwich, Lynn, Yarmouth or London for the Low Countries. Some travelled uneasily by one of the many cargo ships plying the North Sea : before 1687, the mail also went by these private ships—ship letters as they were called : even after the packet service was established, correspondents sometimes preferred this less regular but cheaper method of despatch ; so much so that to regularise it, ship masters were offered ship letter money—a penny for every letter handed over to the post master on arrival. Part of the difficulty in organising postal traffic was the inefficiency of the packet service set up in 1661. An official letter to the agent at Harwich admitted that the English boats compared unfavourably with the Dutch, being "so nasty, ill-provided, and out of order, that we do not only lose many passengers that will not venture with them, but it is a reproach to our nation to have such bad accommodation when our neighbours are so neat and exact in theirs." The institution of an efficient packet service between Harwich and the Brill in 1687 was an event of importance in Anglo-Dutch relations to which too little attention has been accorded by historians.

35

In 1687, a contractor was paid £900 a year to maintain two sixty-ton hoys and one forty-ton hoy to carry mail and passengers between Harwich and the Brill. Each carried a crew of six. Two years later, when war with France broke out, these small hoys were replaced by four larger and better-armed ships carrying fifty men apiece. At this point, William III, who had taken a keen interest in the service between his two Kingdoms, intervened. The King took the sensible if prosaic view that speed to escape and not strength to stay and fight was the first essential in a mail packet. Under his directions, Edmund Drummer, the Surveyor of the Navy, built four smaller, low-built, fast boats for the Post Office. Of course, the sailors grumbled. The bigger ships had promised adventure and prize : the newer boats were uncomfortable in any but the calmest weather, and their ability to show the adversary a clean pair of heels was not an attractive feature to the sailors who preferred the protection of good guns and the chance of a prize. However, they were mollified somewhat by an increase of pay and the new boats were introduced, each with a complement of twenty-one. That the King's policy was sound is proved by the fact that during the next twenty-four years—nineteen of these years of war—only two of this class of boat fell into the hands of the enemy. Some details of one have survived. The packet *Eagle* of 77 tons was built by George Moore at Arundel in Sussex for the Postmaster General in 1703 at a cost of £400 and launched at Shoreham. She was a round-sterned sloop 53 foot long and 18 foot 6 inches beam with "a large Cabbin or State Room, good windlass, suit of masts and yards, caps and cross trees." The State Room was provided with an eye to the accommodation (to say comfort would be to exaggerate) of the distinguished passengers who were carried in both peace and war. For example when Baron Hompesch and Brigadier-General Cadogan are on their way to Holland, orders are given that the packet is to be detained "till Thursday noon, at which time they think to reach Harwich." When M. Rosencrantz, the Danish Envoy, returns to his country, orders are given that no passengers are to be taken on board until he and his suite have been accommodated. As a rule, no passenger was allowed on board without a pass from a Secretary of State : exception was made for shipwrecked mariners, army recruits and junior officers in charge of recruits. Irregular passengers appeared from time to time in spite of this. We hear of Dirck Wolters, an agent carrying " a sealed box directed to a Person of Note in London." No pains are to be spared to discover and apprehend him. As time went on, more and more merchants used the packet service for business trips between London and Amsterdam, and the practice of demanding a pass-port seems to have gone by the board. English visitors usually seem to have made their trips in the Spring to correspond with the tulip season at Haarlem and fine weather. Autumn travellers were less fortunate. John Badcock, a regular visitor to the business house of de Neufville at Amsterdam, writes back to his hosts in November 1749 :

HARWICH
Engraving by de Bry, 17th century

"I am much obliged to you for your civilitys in Holland and your kind
wishes for my good voyage, but was so unlucky by the Packets sailing
sooner than common to lose my Passage, and after waiting at Helvoet
four days to have the worst I ever had."

Boswell describes his departure for the Netherlands in 1763 in his
Life of Dr. Johnson—how he and Johnson set out from London early one
August morning in the Harwich stage coach, how Johnson talked all the
way to Colchester, where they stopped the night at the Inn ; how Johnson
talked the Dutch member of the party into bed, after which he and Boswell
discussed the possibility of Johnson's joining Boswell in Utrecht the
following year (a plan which never materialised). The next day they
reached Harwich : Boswell secured his place in the boat, put his baggage
on board and dined at the Inn with Johnson. After dinner they walked
through the warm summer evening to the Church where Johnson produced his famous "refutation" of Berkeley. Shortly after, the boat sailed.
As it tacked out of the estuary, Boswell watched from the deck for some
time until "rolling his majestic frame in his usual manner" the great man
disappeared from sight.

Constant vigilance was necessary to see that the prime purpose of the
service—the carriage of mail—was not subordinated to other more lucrative and exciting tasks. At Harwich, this duty fell to the agent, who was

37

to see that the packets were properly equipped and victualled, to arrange the order of sailing, to keep the captains to their duty, and generally maintain order and discipline on the station. As soon as the mails from Holland arrived, it was his duty to forward them to London by express ; at best they reached London in eleven hours : at other times there were "vexatious and unexplained delays." Other unexplained delays took place at sea. The captains were strictly forbidden to give chase and only to fight if fight they must, but to avoid this whenever possible and in no case to go in search of adventure or prize. Of course, the instructions were disobeyed, and owing to the facilities offered by the numerous inlets on the East coast for clandestine traffic, smuggling was added to these other illegal pastimes. Packet boats mysteriously disappeared for days together, even when the wind was in the most favourable quarter. In 1704, when the packets were unaccountably irregular, it was alleged that Mr. Vanderpoel, King William's agent at the Brill was actually conniving at these irregular exploits of the packet captains. In the matter of victualling contracts too, the captains and agents combined to line their pockets at the expense of the Postmaster General by grossly exaggerating the list of expenses for which they claimed refund.

As the English National Debt grew rapidly in the early eighteenth century, the merchants and financiers became correspondingly more concerned with the efficiency of the packet service. By 1710 Dutch investors held a considerable stake in the Debt and in the twenties they were deeply involved in the South Sea Bubble. We hear of relays of *pinkjes* (fishing smacks) going out to meet the packet as it approached the Dutch coast in the hope of rushing "hot news"—real or fictitious—to the speculators in the French Coffee House or the Kalverstraat. During the War of the Austrian Succession, the service again became of great importance, not only to speculators in war finance to whom time was money, but to the Government, who, then as later in the Seven Years War, used the packet service to transmit bills of exchange for the payment of British troops on the Continent. For this important function, the Duke of Newcastle availed himself of the services of Sir Joshua Vanneck, the influential Dutch

THE CALM : A SEASHORE SCENE
Oil painting by Charles Brooking, 1723-1759

38

RIVER SCENE WITH BOATS
Oil painting by Willem van de Velde, the younger, 1633-1707

merchant and financier whose office in New Broad Street kept in the closest touch with H.M. Treasury, despatching bills to the Deputy Paymaster at Amsterdam. The difficulty of administering the packet service efficiently in war time brought down criticisms on the Postmaster General's head from every side. The Treasury grumbled because it took so long to transmit bills to Amsterdam. The City financiers were dissatisfied because there was only one London delivery of foreign mail every day. If letters arrived a few minutes after twelve mid-day, they were held up another twenty-four hours. Letters arriving at the Lombard Street Post Office on Saturday from Amsterdam were sometimes not delivered to Lombard Street business houses until Monday evening. To make matters worse, foreign ministers living in London had special deliveries, with the result that foreign nationals often knew of the latest movements of prices on the Amsterdam Bourse long before their English rivals. When one remembers the large Dutch colony which lived in the City, one can imagine the friction caused by such arrangements. The merchants constantly urged reform. At Amsterdam, they said, things were much better managed. Letters were either delivered promptly or might be called for. At Rotterdam the postal authorities allowed an interval for the passage of the mail on to Amsterdam before delivery. Thus, merchants of both cities secured equal treatment. In spite of all their protests the merchants failed to bring about the desired reforms, though the campaign was one more nail in the coffin of an institution falling rapidly into disrepute. The service continued except for intervals caused by war until 1831, when along with other Post Office packet services, it was put out to tender. The General Steam Navigation Company's offer was accepted, with the condition that its vessels should start from the Thames. Shortly afterwards, the packet service to Sweden was transferred to Hull. It was the death-blow to Harwich as a packet station.

The packet service from England to the Netherlands was not the only service to the Continent : there were others from Dover to Calais and Ostend, and from Falmouth to the Groyne. That the Harwich and Brill service must be regarded as the most important was largely due to the fact that the service to France was discontinued during the long periods of the Anglo-French wars, and that the other services were more exposed to the depredations of enemy privateers. It was not brought into existence by the dynastic union of Britain and the Netherlands : it merely reflected the already close economic connections which existed.

The history of the packet service is not without its romance. The State-room of the *Eagle* and her companion ships must have housed many distinguished passengers—the young Cartaret confident, brilliant and successful returning from his diplomatic triumphs in Sweden or setting out for Hanover to ravel and unravel the eternal complications of European diplomacy, fulfilling the destiny he promised himself "to make Kings and Emperors, to maintain the balance of Europe." Townshend, old, tired and disillusioned, coming home to cultivate his turnips after the Dutch manner ; Count Bentinck, the Dutch Ambassador, moving to and fro with his despatch boxes full of shrewd Dutch wisdom about men and affairs ; George II himself going forth to lead his troops in Hanover or hastening back to the gawky Teutonic imitations of French delights at Herrenhausen, accompanied, may be, by Lady Yarmouth ; as well as a whole army of lesser lights. The *Eagle* and her companions carried besides, a succession of fateful despatches—good news of victory at Blenheim or bad of defeat at Fontenoy, or of the progress of the '45 ; Stanhope's orders to the Embassies of Europe, Cartaret's casual asides to the Cabinet from Hanover as he strove to prop up the tottering Hapsburgs against the rising power of France and Prussia ; Newcastle's frantic bribes to the German princes and Pitt's indefatigable stream of orders, promotions and dismissals as he controlled the destinies of British arms in the Seven Years War. Year in, year out, the mail bags aboard the packets carried messages which sealed the fate of Kings, governments and nations ; an hour's delay in sailing or berthing and fortunes might be made in Change Alley or lost on the Amsterdam Bourse. For a century, in fact, the Harwich-Brill packet service was Britain's main link with Europe ; the channel by which our diplomacy was transacted, wars begun, supported and ended, fortunes made and lost, the Funds sustained and the House of Hanover itself supported by foreign alliance and Dutch money.

See you not Learning in his Lookes:
See it more Lively in his Bookes.

HUGO GROTIUS, 1583-1645
Frontispiece to his *De Jure Belli ac Pacis*

HUGO GROTIUS AND THE LAW OF NATIONS

As the new nations of Europe took shape in the sixteenth and seventeenth centuries, they began to reach out in a process of economic expansion. There was competition and there was friction, and from these uneasy processes of adjustment sprang a body of rules to regulate the conduct of international relationships—rules based partly on the special interests, economic and political, of the nations which made them, partly on the general concern of all nations to introduce some measure—however small—of predictability and common standards into the conduct of international affairs. The relations of the two greatest maritime nations of Europe—Holland and Britain—were a specially fruitful source of practical rules and legal doctrines. The history of one of these doctrines—that of the freedom of the seas—is of considerable importance. Let us look forward to the nineteenth century for an authoritative statement of it—to 1817, when Lord Stowell gave it as his opinion that "All nations being equal, all have an equal right to the uninterrupted use of the unappropriated parts of the ocean for their navigation."

It was the burial, long overdue, of a doctrine of maritime sovereignty which had been dead for a hundred years and moribund for fifty before that, and its official replacement by the doctrine of the freedom of the seas.

During the nineteenth century that doctrine came to be regarded as specially a British conception, bound up indissolubly with the spread of British dominion over the map of the world. In fact, the doctrine of the freedom of the seas—the doctrine that every nation has equal rights of navigation and fishing on the high seas—was a Dutch doctrine, the work of the great Dutch jurist Hugo Grotius, who, in the early seventeenth century, preached it on behalf of his seafaring nation in flat defiance of the other three important maritime powers, Spain, Portugal—and Britain herself. For in spite of all that has been written and said about the spacious days of Queen Elizabeth, Jacobean England was still parochially-minded, with a sea-borne trade that was only just beginning to stretch its sea-legs ; militarily Britain was on the defensive, and her ideas on international usage lagged a long way behind the bold but intermittent voyages of piracy and discovery of Elizabeth's seadogs.

Much has been written about Grotius, "the founder of modern international law," but it has not always been made clear how essential was the relationship between Grotius's ideas and the practical needs of the Dutch merchants and seagoing traders of his time, nor how it came about that a doctrine which suited the Dutch in one century came to suit the British in the next. The fact is that Grotius's opinions on international law were neither academic nor wholly altruistic (though neither were they venal or purely nationalist). They were conditioned by the economic system under which the Dutch traded and became a wealthy colonial power. In particular, his doctrine of the freedom of the seas reflects the interests of Dutch shipping and trade in 1600 as accurately as the later British doctrine of the Right of Search reflected the needs of British naval strategy. That Grotius's writings give the impression of being written *sub specie aeternitatis* is perhaps partly due to the fact that, being a good lawyer, he chose his examples and proofs from the safe distance of classical antiquity, avoiding the thornier paths of contemporary happenings. The picture of Grotius as an academic recluse is quite false. He was, in fact, a man of great energy, practical and versatile, a practising lawyer, a great classical scholar, poet and philologist, theologian, administrator, politician and diplomat.

During the Twelve Years Truce with Spain, Oldenbarneveldt, Grand Pensionary of Holland, appointed Grotius Pensionary of Rotterdam. Later he visited England to help in settling disputes which had arisen between the English and Dutch East India Companies. It was partly these

WEST INDIA HOUSE, AMSTERDAM
Engraving, 1693

contacts with England which led him into serious troubles at home. In Holland the great dispute was raging between the orthodox Calvinists (the predestinarians or Contra-Remonstrants) led by Gomarus, and the Remonstrants, who wanted to soften the rigours of predestinarian orthodoxy, led by Arminius. Grotius, a tolerant and reasonable man in an age which favoured neither tolerance nor reason, inclined to the views of Arminius and supported him in discussions with James I and the Archbishop of Canterbury. As a result of these discussions, Grotius drafted a Resolution, calling a Conference to settle the religious disputes in the Netherlands and empowering the Dutch municipalities to set up militia. Grotius had the misfortune to belong by temperament and conviction to the wrong side—the side which was doomed to defeat at Dort. He was imprisoned along with Oldenbarneveldt but escaped his fate of execution. Everyone knows the story of his escape from the prison at Loevestein in a trunk—a tale worthy of Dumas : from there he escaped to Antwerp and Paris. His later days were spent in the diplomatic service of Sweden. His life, then, can scarcely be described as cloistered or uneventful : Grotius was sufficiently a man of the world to reconcile his conscience with the legal requirements of his country's trade, but not worldly enough to make a success of a career amidst the sordid intrigues of seventeenth-century Court diplomacy.

To understand how revolutionary Grotius's doctrines were, we need only examine briefly his contemporaries' ideas on maritime rights. The sixteenth century was an age of "closed waters," when states were in the habit of claiming absolute sovereignty over their local seas. Venice, for example, claimed sovereignty over the Adriatic ; Britain claimed to rule the seas which surrounded the British Isles, while Denmark and Sweden disputed rule in the Baltic. Even the advent of longer voyages did not by any means spell the end of the old theory. The great Colonial Powers of the sixteenth century, Spain and Portugal, continued to apply it to their overseas possessions, the Spaniards claiming the Pacific and the Gulf of Mexico, Portugal the South Atlantic and the Indian Ocean, basing their claim partly on conquest, partly on discovery and occupation and partly on Papal award. Foreigners were therefore excluded from these waters. It was the intrusion of the Dutch, thrusting South to Africa and eastwards to Mauritius then to Java and Moluccas, which put an end to the old ideas : the test came in 1602, when a Dutch ship belonging to the East Indies Company captured a Portuguese galleon, the *Catherine*, in the Malacca Straits. Grotius was apparently retained as counsel for the East Indies Company, and was largely responsible for securing the forfeit and confiscation of the goods aboard the galleon in the Amsterdam Court of Admiralty.

During the negotiations which led to the Twelve Years Truce with Spain, the Spaniards tried to persuade the Dutch to renounce their claims to trade in the East and West Indies. It was then, in 1608, that Grotius expanded and published his earlier brief under the title *The Freedom of the Seas or the Right that Belongs to the Dutch to take part in the East Indian Trade*. What was not known until 1868 was that this was only an isolated chapter of a much greater work— the *De Jure Praedae*—(*Concerning the Law of Prize*).

In the *Mare Liberum*, Grotius was mainly concerned to refute the Spanish and Portuguese claims to sovereignty over those tropical seas into which his countrymen were penetrating, but the denial carried with it implications which were designed to alter the whole theory of maritime rights—and amongst those affected the British were not the least concerned. Grotius sets out the quarrel succintly :

"Between us and the Spaniards the following points are in dispute : Can the vast, the boundless sea be the appanage of one Kingdom alone, and it not the greatest ? Can any one Nation have the right to prevent other nations which so desire from selling to one another, from bartering with one another, actually from communicating with one another ? Can any Nation give away what it never owned, or discover what already belonged to someone else ? Does a manifest injustice of long standing create a specific right ?"

44

DUTCH EAST INDIAMEN
Etching by Wenceslaus Hollar, 1607-1677

He then proceeds to show that the Portuguese have no right to sovereignty over the East Indies either by discovery, by war, by occupation
or by Papal Donation. Therefore, he continues :

". . . freedom of trade is based on a primitive right of Nations which
has a natural and permanent cause; and so that right cannot be destroyed,
or at all events it may not be destroyed except by the consent of all
Nations."

Nevertheless, if the United Provinces were to be driven into war by
the injustice of their enemies, the justice of their cause would give them
hope and confidence in the final outcome :

"Therefore, if it be necessary, Arise, O Nation unconquered on the
sea, and fight boldly, not only for your own liberation but for that of
the human race. Nor let it fright thee that their fleet is winged, each ship
with an hundred oars. The sea whereon it sails will have none of it.
And though the prows bear figures threatening to cast rocks such as
Centaurs throw, thou shalt find them but hollow planks and painted
terrors. 'Tis his cause that makes or mars a soldier's strength. If the
cause be not just, shame strikes the weapon from his hands."

So far as colonial trade was concerned, the British vested interests
were as yet not extensive, though, as we have seen, Grotius was sent to
England to help mediate in minor disputes. There was, however, a fruitful
field of controversy and dissension nearer home—the fisheries off the
English and Scottish coasts which were largely exploited by Dutch fishermen. Here Grotius applied the same principle as in navigation, namely,
that "it remains free and open to all." And in the strained atmosphere of

45

English constitutional affairs, his further remarks on the right to levy revenue could hardly be regarded by the Parliamentarians as doing anything but adding insult to injury :

"Similarly, revenues levied on maritime fisheries are held to belong to the Crown, but they do not bind the sea itself or the fisheries, but only the persons engaged in fishing. Wherefore subjects for whom a state or ruler is by common consent competent to make laws, will perhaps be compelled to bear such charges, but so far as other persons are concerned, the right of fishing ought everywhere to be exempt from tolls, lest a servitude be imposed upon the sea, which is not susceptible to a servitude."

In other words, James I might tax English fishermen, but not Dutch.

The implications of Grotius's theory did not go unnoticed in England where Selden produced his *Mare Clausum* to defend the old theory and especially to refute Grotius's claims for the Dutch fishermen. (Selden's work was written in 1617 but not published until 1635.) Selden's thesis was twofold : first, "that the sea, by the law of nature or nations, is not common to all men, but capable of private dominion or property as well as the land" ; and secondly, "that the King of Great Britain is Lord of the sea flowing about, as an inseparable appendant of the British Empire." Since the Scottish fisheries were likewise in bondage to the Dutch, we find William Welwood, a lawyer of Aberdeen University, expressing views similar to Selden's in his *Abridgement of all the Sea-Lawes* (1613). What was the result of this conflict between the new theory and the old ? It was, briefly, that for some years the English won a victory for the old theory of maritime sovereignty. They compelled the Dutch to take out English licences to fish off the English coasts. In 1636, the Dutch tried to ignore the demand and fish without a licence : they were attacked and compelled to pay £30,000 for leave to remain. On the whole the British succeeded in enforcing their sovereignty by making the Dutch accord honours of the flag (symbolising maritime sovereignty). The Dutch had to acknowledge the obligation in the two treaties of Westminster (1654 and 1674) and in the Treaty of Breda in 1667. But the conflict had already largely lost its point, and towards the end of the century, events moved rapidly. By 1667, a turning point had been reached in Anglo-Dutch relations ; the colonial disputes were largely settled, and the way was clear for an alliance which began in 1689 and lasted for two generations, first under William III and then under Marlborough and Heinsius. By 1700, the old theory of maritime sovereignty was dwindling away as British ocean-going trade extended as widely as the Dutch trade had done a century earlier. British fishing vessels were roaming as far into foreign waters as the Dutch, and the old parochialism was out-moded. The doctrine of freedom of the seas was a doctrine appropriate to an expanding national economy and as Britain, learning from the Dutch, came to contest the Dutch monopoly of world trade and passed to an economic offensive against the vested economic

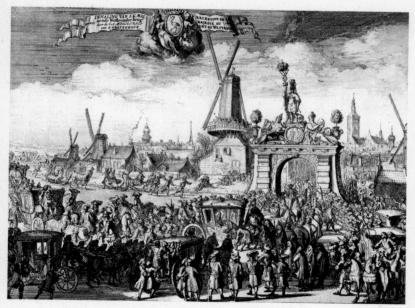

ENTRY OF WILLIAM III INTO THE HAGUE
Engraving from Arnoud Leers' *Komste van Willem III in Holland*, 1691

rights of the other powers, it became expedient for Britain to take over the Dutch doctrine of the *mare liberum*.

By the time Grotius's name was fully restored to honour in his own country, his theory, devised to justify and extend his nation's commerce and navigation, had been appropriated by another power, and the Dutch were shaping for a neutral or at most passive role in European politics. In the eighteenth century one of the most powerful factors which shaped the development of international law was the jostling of the Dutch by the main belligerent powers, Britain and France. Under this stimulus, the Dutch—and principally the great jurist, Bynkershoek—built upon Grotius's foundations (or upon none at all) a whole theory of the laws of neutrality. In a problem which was a brutally practical one, theory was not of much assistance. Grotius, in his *De Jure Belli ac Pacis* had merely commented that the duty of a neutral was not to help a belligerent carrying on an unjust war, nor to hinder a belligerent carrying on a just war : and in doubtful cases "to act alike to both sides, in permitting transit, in shipping provisions to the respective armies, and in not assisting persons besieged." In translating this into practice, the main problems to be solved were ; first, what goods might Dutch ships supply to a belligerent and secondly (since the Dutch were a great carrying power) what belligerent goods might be carried in bottoms ? As regards contraband, Grotius's analysis remained and goods were classed as (*a*) objects of use in war only ;

47

(*b*) goods useless in war, such as luxury articles ; (*c*) money, provisions, ships, etc., which were useful in peace and war. But as to definition, opinions differed as they have always continued to differ, and practice varied according to requirements and convenience. Not unnaturally, Bynkershoek devoted his efforts to limiting the range of prohibited articles.

In the matter of the carriage of enemy goods, Grotius had held to the old theory that all enemy goods were liable to seizure. But after the middle of the seventeenth century, the Dutch evolved the doctrine of "Free ships, free goods" which went to the opposite extreme, and between 1650 and 1700 they persuaded Spain, Portugal, France, Sweden and England to grant the privilege in no fewer than twelve treaties. Britain never regarded herself as bound by these ; and went on seizing enemy goods while releasing the ships with payment of freight—a policy which brought her into collision with the neutrals in 1780, when the first Armed Neutrality put forward the immunity of belligerent cargoes in neutral ships as one of its main doctrines. A Dutch convoy was captured and taken into Spithead and Dutch protests answered with the threat that all foreign vessels found assisting the enemy with warlike stores might be considered lawful prize. The last Anglo-Dutch war broke out in December 1780.

In as much as law proceeds from the successful rather than the unsuccessful members of society, it is not surprising that international law, like national law, should reflect the anxiety of the acquisitive either for what they have acquired or for what they hope to acquire. The view of commerce as something necessarily tainted, a breeding ground of dishonesty or oppression, found few adherents between the sixteenth and nineteenth centuries ; for the Early Fathers were gone and *Das Capital* was not yet come. In common with thousands of civilised and religious men, British and Dutch, Grotius regarded the furthering of his peoples' trade as an object worthy of his best exertions. And indeed it must have been difficult to see what was wrong with a campaign that brought neither the chain of debt which the medieval money-lender had loaded on agricultural society, nor the squalor, vice and misery which nineteenth century industry brought (or at any rate, multiplied) in London or Liverpool or a dozen other cities. Spices, silks, tea, coffee, tobacco and rice—these were the harmless gifts which the merchants offered to eke out a monotonous diet, to add colour to a drab scene. For the long dreariness of India's problems was still in the future, and if a conscience here and there rebelled at the tales of horror from the slave-ships that carried their human cargoes to the New World, were there not hundreds of negro servants in Western Europe, as well-fed and contented as Francis Barber ("the ladies' favourite" of Boswell) whom Johnson schooled and treated a good deal better than many men treated their sons or wards ? But when we have made every allowance for an age which, very sensibly, made the tradesmen's case its own, it would be foolish to deny a nobler strain in Grotius when, in the introduction to his great *De Jure Belli ac Pacis* he writes :

GERARDUS MERCATOR NATUS
RUPELMUNDÆ III NON.MARTII ANNO
CIƆIƆXII.VIXIT ANN.LXXXII.M.VIII.D.
XXVI:DENATUS IV NON.DECEMBRIS
ANNO CIƆIƆXCIV.

IUDOCUS HONDIUS NATUS IN
PAGO FLANDRIÆ DICTO WACKENE XVI
KALEND.NOVEMBRIS ANNO CIƆIƆLXIII:
VIXIT ANN.XLVII.M.VII.D.XXIX:DENAT:
US XIV KAL.MARTII ANNO CIƆIƆCXII.

MERCATOR AND HONDIUS
Coloured engraved frontispiece to Mercator's World Atlas, 1612

WILLIAM III LANDING AT BRIXHAM, DEVON, NOVEMBER 5TH, 1688
Detail from a contemporary oil painting by an unknown Dutch artist

"A citizen who conducts himself in accordance with the laws of his country does not thereby behave foolishly, although, in consequence of these laws, he must deny himself certain things which might be of advantage to him personally. Similarly, a nation cannot reasonably be considered foolish that does not so strongly emphasise its own interests as to tread under foot the common laws of States and Nations. The cases are identical, for a citizen who for his direct advantage infringes the social laws of his country destroys the foundations of his higher interests and at the same time those of his descendants. The nation that opposes the law of nature and the law of nations overthrows the bulwark of its future peace."

In the *Mare Liberum* we have seen Grotius justifying the right of an offended nation to wage war ; not that, in an age which took for granted the unrestrained right of waging war, many would have been found to quibble over that. The novelty in Grotius's doctrines was that they attacked that unrestrained right and limited it strictly to an instrument for use against 'guilty' States. Like the founders of the League of Nations, Grotius wanted a world Court of Justice ; with more practical wisdom than they showed he recommended also that it should have executive powers to carry out its sentences.

No account of Grotius which leaves out some reference to his theological works could be anything but misleading. Grotius himself can hardly have been rejoiced by the apparently meagre success of his efforts to bridge the gap in Holland between the Calvinists and the extreme Arminians like Episcopius. Yet in Scotland, his *De Veritate Religione Christianae*, the *De Satisfactione Christi* and his commentaries on various books of the Bible, were reading common to Episcopalians and Presbyterians ; and while some of the latter regarded him as 'Tridentine poperie' and some of the former thought him a Socinian, both sides acknowledged his eminence. Slowly, the leaven of his reasonableness worked and the comparative tolerance of the eighteenth century owed much to him. Samuel Johnson took great comfort from Grotius's steady Christian faith. "Grotius," said Johnson, "was not a recluse, but a man of the world who certainly had no bias to the side of religion. Grotius was an acute man, a lawyer, a man accustomed to examine evidence, and he was convinced." And in 1777 he recommended to the Archbishop of Canterbury as a candidate for entrance to the Charterhouse, one de Groot—a man "old, poor and infirm in a great degree." But he had another claim "to which no scholar can refuse attention." He was :

". . . by several descents the nephew of Hugo Grotius ; of him from whom perhaps every man of learning has learnt something. Let it not be said" (concluded Johnson's letter to the Rector of Lambeth) "that in any lettered country a nephew of Grotius asked a charity and was refused."

To the Archbishop's credit, let it be said that it was not.

MILTON AND THE DUTCH BACKGROUND

The works of John Milton, and especially *Paradise Lost*, afford the most startling—and perhaps the most controversial—example of the influence of contemporary Dutch thought on English literature in the seventeenth century. Two late nineteenth century critics—Edmund Gosse and the historian Edmundson—went to great pains to prove the extent of Milton's indebtedness to the Dutch poet Joost van den Vondel, Gosse in an essay called *Vondel and Milton* (*Studies in the Literature of Northern Europe*, 1879) and Edmundson in his study *Milton and Vondel*, published six years later. Although the two critics disagreed on details, they had a good deal of ground in common. They both noted the probable debt which Milton owed to the Latin poem of Hugo Grotius, *Adamus Exul*, published in 1601. Both seized on the evidence that Milton took lessons in Dutch from Roger Williams (the founder of the State of Rhode Island) who "formed an intimate acquaintance" with Milton during his stay in London from 1651 to 1654. These are certainly years during which Milton, as Latin Secretary to the Council of State, had much to do with the Dutch. The war in the Channel led to constant negotiations, and Milton was brought into touch with many eminent Dutchmen who came to London as special envoys, among them Pensionary Cats. He was apparently allowed a weekly table for the entertainment of these distinguished foreigners. At the same time he was engaged in bitter controversy with two opponents in Holland—Salmasius, Professor at Leyden, and Morus, a theological Professor (of Scottish extraction) at Middelburg. Milton's replies to the enemy pamphleteers brought him fame in the United Provinces. He was at the same time in constant contact with agents in Holland who kept him informed on Dutch affairs ; John Durie at Amsterdam, Theodore Haak, a Dutchman, John Pell, an English professor of mathematics at Amsterdam, and Ulac, the Hague publisher, who printed with cheerful impartiality for both Milton and Salmasius. Years earlier, in 1638, Milton setting out for Italy, travelled through Paris, and asked the English Ambassador to give him an introduction to Grotius, then exiled to the French capital by the malice of the extreme Calvinist and Orangist party in his own country. "Grotius," says Milton's nephew, Edward Phillips, "took Milton's visit kindly, and gave him entertainment suitable to his worth and the high commendations he had heard of him." Grotius, as has already been noted, was the friend and protector of Vondel, who, about the time of Milton's meeting at Paris, dedicated to him his tragedy, *Gysbrecht van Amstel*.

Against this kind of background, Edmundson—the more accurate if less attractive of the two—sought to demonstrate the debt which Milton's *Paradise Lost* and *Paradise Regained* owed to Vondel's *Lucifer*. Edmundson himself was satisfied that he had established the certainty that Milton was generally in debt to the Dutch poet, and the strong probability that he

HET
PARADYS VERLOOREN
HELDENDICHT,
GESCHETST NA'T ENGELSCH
VAN IOHN MILTON.
DOOR
L.P.

T'AMSTELDAM by EVERT VISSCHER, 1730.

I. C. Philips inv. et fecit. 1729.

MILTON's *PARADISE LOST*
Engraved frontispiece to a Dutch edition. Amsterdam, 1730

borrowed particular ideas, and even particular phrases, images and similes from him. And there the matter rested : Milton's relationship to Vondel was to Edmundson, *A Curiosity of Literature*. The implication that the greatest epic poem in the language was not essentially original did not go unchallenged; but it is not necessary to revive a controversy which brought no one any particular profit and which, in the absence of any more concrete evidence, must necessarily remain largely a matter of opinion. There is, however, another side to this story which has never been adequately told : and vast though its ramifications are, it can at least be touched on here.

Edmundson himself regarded his discovery, as we have said, as an historical curiosity : but historical curiosities have a habit of appearing less curious, though not necessarily less remarkable, when they are seen in their historical context. This one is no exception. Gosse and Edmundson both treated their subject in isolation because (I think) in common with many critics and historians of their time, they were not much interested in the complex of religious and intellectual relationships which formed its background; with a confident Victorian dislike for theological controversy, they could not believe that the dispute between the men who believed in predestination and the men who clung to free will could really have been any more to the men of those times than the tedious and regrettable business that it seemed to be to the enlightened onlooker of the Victorian Age. Yet a dispute which tore society in Holland and in Scotland into two halves, which helped to bring revolution, regicide and fratricide in England, which brought death to Oldenbarneveldt and de Witt, and exile to Grotius, cannot be dismissed as a lamentable historical nuisance. Nor is it possible to see the relationship between the two poets in its true perspective without some reference to the theological background common to both. To the humanist Vondel as to the humanist Milton, the idea of predestination—the theology of the great majority of English and Dutch Calvinists—was repulsive. This hatred of the doctrine which denied any freedom of choice to man is fundamental in Vondel's writing and it brought upon him and his group the implacable enmity of the extreme Calvinists. In England there was hardly the same aptitude for isolating theological topics nor the same predilection for purely theological disputation as there was in Holland or in Scotland; the quarrel became overlaid with other things—with arguments about ritual and vestments, about church government and episcopacy, about royalism and republicanism and even tonnage and poundage, with the fear always in the background that Anglicanism might lapse into Popery. These things have tended to obscure the important fact that Milton was (or at least became) theologically an Arminian, that though a Puritan, he subscribed to a creed which had he been a Dutchman would have subjected him to the Calvinist persecution which Grotius and Vondel had to suffer. A glance at Vondel and some of those who were of his way of thinking, and at their contacts with England make the comparison clearer.

JOOST VAN DEN VONDEL, 1587-1679
Engraving from the British Museum copy of Vondel's *Lucifer*

During his long life of ninety-one years, Vondel numbered amongst his friends many of the greatest of the poets and scholars of his age, an age which in a sudden brilliant efflorescence produced a richer crop of genius than any other period in Dutch history. But diverse as were the views and characters of these men and women of Vondel's circle, they all found themselves in some measure in opposition to the ideas of the religious party which won the day at the Synod of Dort. Whatever the value of the Calvinistic faith may have been in hardening and focussing the resistance to Spain, it nevertheless evoked an instinctive antipathy amongst important intellectual sections of Dutch society. The tyranny of the pulpit threatened freedom of thought and expression, and in the struggle for power between the secular and church authorities which raged in the first quarter of the seventeenth century, Grotius and Vondel ranged themselves instinctively behind Oldenbarneveldt. The whole literary movement was opposed to the pretensions of the Gomarist party (Gomarus was the leader of the Dutch High Calvinists) because those pretensions spelt the end of the free Renaissance spirit, of the reasonable influence of Erasmus, of classical learning, the end of the freedom of spirit to which they attached supreme importance. No one epitomised these influences and aspirations better than Peter Cornelizoon Hooft, Sheriff of Muiden, humanist, poet and historian, the patron and leader of the group of poets which became known as the *Muidenkring*.

Hooft represents in Dutch literature that combination of Latin and Northern influences which Moreelse and Honthorst represent in art and which by the second quarter of the seventeenth century was being supplanted by a more homely and native civilisation. Like them he spent his formative years in Italy. What Raphael was to the artists, Tasso was to the young poet. After he returned home, his picturesque castle at Muiden, with its drawbridge and pointed turrets looking out over the Zuider Zee, its trees and orchards, became the meeting-place and the retreat of Vondel, of Anna and Tesselschade Visscher, of Huygens, of Samuel Coster, Barlaeus and many others. Hooft managed to achieve a remarkably satisfactory synthesis of the many diverse elements which went to make up his character. In his poems as in his *History*, we find the same sanity and reasonableness, a stoical serenity that rebukes all violence and fanaticism, Catholic as well as Calvinist, mob hysteria as well as individual bigotry.

With Constantijn Huygens it was very different. Huygens was a compound of many influences, religious and social. He was a strong Protestant, in some ways very like an English Puritan, at the same time a diplomat and courtier speaking French and writing French poems, and corresponding with Corneille and Balzac. Yet these elements did not harmonise as they did in Hooft : where there was ease in the one, there was hypersensitiveness and harshness in the other. In many ways, Huygens resembles John Donne, whose poems he attempted to translate. Many of his own poems display the features we associate with Donne's metaphysical poems —the obscurity, the unexpected metaphor or allusion, the conceit, the use of the grotesque, the juxtaposition of the spiritual and the sensual— all these things are common to both. Milton may well have seen in the *Muidenkring* a foreshadowing of the conflict between Puritanism and Humanism which was later to dominate his own personality and his own great epic.

Vondel's friendship with Grotius has already been mentioned. Grotius was the unquestioned leader of the intellectual opposition to the high Calvinist party in Holland ; for his support of their political leader, Oldenbarneveldt, he was rewarded with imprisonment and exile. Vondel's indignation found expression in a play—the *Palamedes*—in which, under the form of a Greek drama, he satirised the conduct of Oldenbarneveldt's persecutors. Through Grotius, Vondel was also connected with Gerard Vossius, another of the leaders of the moderate Arminians, and the father of Isaac Vossius, the strange eccentric who later became a Canon of Windsor. Grotius and Vossius themselves form a valuable link with the English Arminians, and especially with Lancelot Andrewes. Andrewes, successively Bishop of Chichester, Ely and Winchester, one of the noblest figures of seventeenth century Anglicanism, and after Hooker the greatest

THE CASTLE OF MUIDEN
Oil painting by Jan Abrahamsz Beerstraaten, 1658

defender of the Anglican compromise, was universally respected in an age when Bishops were anything but popular even with the devout Anglican layman. Perhaps it was through his offices that Laud, in 1629, presented Gerard Vossius and Isaac Casaubon to Canonries at Canterbury. Vossius returned to Amsterdam four years later, though he maintained a long correspondence with some of the leading Anglicans, lay and clerical, of the day—with Lord Herbert of Cherbury, with Laud, Andrewes, Ussher, Sterne and Wren. The learned Casaubon, also befriended by Andrewes, stayed on.

We must not push the thesis too far, but these facts show that there was a close connection between the English Arminians and the considerable body of civilised people in Holland who were opposed to the dogmatic predestinarianism of the high Calvinists. It is, moreover, difficult to avoid the conclusion that these men were in fact seeking a *via media* in religion on the lines of the Anglican compromise. If Henry IV had succeeded in the attempt in France, Casaubon might have been the Hooker of France. If Oldenbarneveldt had succeeded, Grotius or Vossius might have performed a similar office for Holland. The moderate Dutch Arminians saw religion in their own country caught up in endless quarrels about a point in doctrine ; it is little wonder that they should have been attracted by the broad humanity of Andrewes' kind of churchmanship.

But the spirit of Erasmus was not easily to be conjured back to the land of his birth, where the long struggle against bigotry had temporarily begotten a local spirit of persecution.

We must turn back for a moment to Vondel to see how he fits into this history of controversy. Vondel would no doubt have welcomed some reasonable solution of the theological deadlock but he too was provoked to violence by the rigid dogmatism of his opponents. In his *Decretum Horribile* he attacked the doctrine of predestination, declaring that Calvin was a greater slanderer of God than Servetus (whom Calvin had condemned as a heretic) and denouncing Gomarus. I quote a passage which clearly shows the horror Vondel experienced when he surveyed the conclusions to which his opponent's doctrine led:

"God snatches the innocent child even from its mother's breast, and hurls it into the everlasting fire! O Gulf! O yawning grave! Where shall I escape your stench? And dares this monster strike his claws into Servetus and dash him to the ground as a slanderer of God, after this scandalous book had spewed its loathsome curse in the face of heaven? Where am I? Under the light of lamps that God has kindled or under Lucifer, in the black realm of smoke? Is this the Providence of which the chosen vessel of God spoke? Is this the consolation of the sick? Is this the treasure Christ has brought to light? . . .

"Is God the crocodile who devours as a luxury the new-born child, on the bank of the Nile? Is God a hypocrite who welcomes the Star in the East with chant and organ and paints the streets of Bethlehem, with the colours of murder? . . . Is God a Moloch, a stranger to mercy, who takes the offered child in his red-hot arms and gives at the breast to drink of fire and flaming oil? But that would be an act of mercy, a sleeping draught. The child would rest, released from terror . . ." (The translation is that used by Professor Grierson in his *Cross Currents in English Literature in the Seventeenth Century*.)

The relevance of this to Milton and Vondel has not perhaps been fully appreciated. Edmundson, for example, writes ". . . it is surely a wonderful coincidence, and one that points to a curious affinity between the two poets, that at the very time when the Englishman was, after long years of musing and preparation, slowly girding himself to the task, which he had set before him from his youth, of writing a great poem upon the subject of the Fall of Man, his Dutch contemporary should produce a drama, the finest, in many respects, of all his works, which covers the same ground, and that, again, immediately before Milton had reached that portion of his epic which dwells upon the actual Fall and its consequences, Vondel should likewise have chosen this precise episode as the subject for dramatic treatment." But is it such a coincidence? Here were three men—Milton, Vondel, Grotius—all of them passionately concerned with one of the greatest theological disputes in Christian history, a dispute which itself largely turned upon a particular view of the fall of Adam.

Is it so strange that all three should have taken the story of Adam to illustrate and dramatise the theme of the freedom of the human will?

The theme of Milton, Vondel and Grotius alike was that a man was left a way of salvation from a state of sin which was itself the result of his own free will.

To Milton, reason was the supreme gift of God to man and reason meant freedom of will. That is the main theme of *Paradise Lost* viewed as a didactic poem and it occupies pretty well the whole of Book V in the form of a dialogue between Raphael and Adam. It is also one of the main themes of the *De Doctrina*. It is perhaps not irrelevant to recall at this point that as a young man, Milton composed an elegy on the death of Lancelot Andrewes, the friend of Grotius and Vossius.

Another point which was not mentioned by Gosse or Edmundson but which helps to complete the mosaic, should not be overlooked. That is the work of the Dutch scholar, Francis Junius of Leyden, who was in England between 1620 and 1651 and again from 1675 to 1677. Junius had devoted himself to the study of the old Teutonic languages and especially to Anglo-Saxon. Through his brother-in-law, Gerard Vossius, Junius was known to Bishop Ussher who gave him the M.S. (now in the Bodleian) of the so-called 'Caedmon' poems. These consisted of paraphrases of Genesis, Exodus and Daniel, and three poems on the lamentations of the Fallen Angels, the "Harrowing of Hell" and the temptation; the researches of the Dutch scholar were certainly available to Milton amongst the sources for his epic.

These historical and biographical data which form the background of *Paradise Lost* do not solve the problem of Milton's "debt" to Vondel; they rather indicate a new approach to the question, by suggesting that in both England and Holland there was a reaction against high Calvinist doctrine amongst poets, scholars and men of letters which took a strikingly similar form; by suggesting that it is unlikely that the two groups were unconscious of the way in which their opposite numbers were thinking and by showing that in fact there were intimate contacts between them. Previously the question at issue has been one if not of plagiarism, at least something approaching it; but when the subject is treated, not in isolation but in its historical context, it becomes much less a question of analysing direct borrowings and more one of assessing how far each poem represents a humanistic reaction against a theological doctrine incompatible with the humanist's view of human dignity and spiritual freedom.

It will be seen that the relationship between Milton and Vondel cannot be considered apart from its context; it is only a single thread in a much broader fabric of intellectual relationships and collective sympathies, a fabric in which the intellectual and theological fashions of England and the Netherlands were inseparably interwoven.

ENGLISH INFLUENCES IN DUTCH LITERATURE

The coming of the new Europe and the formation of national states did not extinguish immediately the cosmopolitan spirit of the Middle Ages. Amongst scholars and men of letters especially, it lived on. Wars there had always been : the kings, princes and barons of medieval Europe had always had their marauding expeditions and military adventures, and the scholars largely ignored the process by which those expeditions had become national conflicts. This was especially true of England and the Netherlands, which offered hospitality to each others scholars even when the struggle for commercial and maritime supremacy was at its most bitter. Scholars and artists moved from one country to the other as easily as a man might go from Kent to Surrey. *Everyman,* the finest of all the morality plays, was once thought to be an English version of a slightly earlier Dutch play, but the reverse opinion is now generally held. A hundred years after Erasmus of Rotterdam kept at Queen's for the last time, there were Dutch Canons at Canterbury and Windsor, English and Scottish professors and students at Amsterdam and Leyden, Dutch painters at the English Court, English poets and philosophers at Amsterdam and the Hague. The obstacles of distance and language were overcome or ignored in a way which to-day seems quite remarkable. Even war did little to disturb the calm of these colonies which dwelt among strange peoples. Some of the emigrants were, it is true, refugees blown to a foreign shore by the ill-wind of persecution, but there were many other voluntary exiles : and in those days of leisured and casual diplomacy, it is perhaps natural that many of those who mingled and enriched the literature of both countries should have been ambassadors or diplomatists. Towards the end of the sixteenth century, for example, Dirk (Theodore) Rodenburgh, the Dutch poet and dramatist, visited England as an emissary of the Dutch Government, and came under the influence of the Elizabethan dramatists. Amongst other things, Rodenburgh translated into Dutch Sidney's *Apologie for Poetrie* and Cyril Tourneur's *Revenger's Tragedy.* In 1600, the Pensionary Jacob Cats visited England for the first time, going to Cambridge and Oxford. Cats became a well-known figure in this country and when he later became Ambassador of the United Provinces in England, he was knighted by Charles I. Cats, let it be said, was no mere rustic wit : he was a man of wide culture, a capable jurist and a tolerably good administrator. Constantijn Huygens——diplomat, administrator and poet—also came to England frequently and was the friend of John Donne, whose verse he attempted, with more courage than success, to translate. His own verse was considerably influenced by the example of the English "metaphysicals." His son, Constantijn, accompanied William of Orange to England as Secretary, and paints a vivid picture of English Society in his lively and caustic *Journal.* From the English side, Christopher Marlowe, Ben Jonson, Giles Fletcher

TWO SKATERS
Pen and wash drawing by Henrik Avercamp, 1585—c.1663

and John Donne all visited the Low Countries. Later in the century, Sir William Temple was active in stimulating Dutch interest in English writing while he was Minister to the States General. His essay *Of Poetry* seems to have commanded as wide a public in the Netherlands as his *Observations on the United Provinces* did in England. Temple's mission was carried on by the Whig exiles, by Burnet, the confidant and adviser of both William and Mary, by the Earl of Shaftesbury, and by John Locke. From 1684 to 1688, Locke lived at Amsterdam and Utrecht, presiding precariously (as Mynheer van der Linden) over his Lantern Club, and periodically fleeing extradition along the dark alleys and by the canals of the Dutch cities. The diplomat replaced the refugee once more in the person of Matthew Prior, who became Secretary to William the Third's Ambassador at the Hague, and an Interim Gentleman of the Bedchamber to the King. Prior once described himself, perhaps over-modestly, as "only a poet by accident." It is true that he was also a diligent and by no means unsuccessful diplomat—witness his part in the negotiations leading up to the Treaty of Ryswick ; while

> "In the vile Utrecht Treaty, too,
> Poor man ! He found enough to do."

But besides being part-author of what was sometimes called "Matt's Peace," Prior was also a witty and delightful lyric poet. His poem *The Secretary*, in which he describes the pleasure of life at the Hague atones in some measure for Andrew Marvell's rudeness.

> "With labour assiduous due pleasure I mix,
> And in one day atone for the business of six,
> In a little Dutch chaise, on a Saturday night,
> On my left hand my Horace, a nymph on my right :
> No memoirs to compose, and no post-boy to move,
> That on Sunday may hinder the softness of love ;
> For her, neither visits, nor parties at tea,
> Nor the long-winded cant of a dull refugee :
> This night and the next shall be hers, shall be mine ;
> To good or ill-fortune the third we resign.
> Thus scorning the world, and superior to Fate
> I drive in my car in professional state ;
> So with Phia thro' Athens Pisistratus rode,
> Men thought her Minerva and him a new God.
> But why should I stories of Athens rehearse,
> Where people knew love and were partial to verse,
> Since none can with justice my pleasures oppose
> In Holland half-drowned in int'rest and prose ?
> By Greece and past ages what need I be tried
> When the Hague and the present are both by my side ?
> And is it enough for the joys of the day
> To think what Anacreon or Sappho would say,
> When good Vandergoes and his provident Vrouw,
> As they gaze on my triumph, so freely allow,
> That search all the Province, you'll find no man dar is
> So blest as the *Englishen Heer Secretar* is ?

Continuous intercourse brought it about that by 1700 there was a considerable and intelligent interest amongst the Dutch reading public in English writing and in the potentialities of the English language as a medium of expression, an interest which was stimulated by the great printing and book-selling trade which had grown up in seventeenth century Holland, following on Blaeu's improvements in printing technique.

WINDSOR CASTLE
Pen drawing by J. Hoefnagel, 1571

Many famous English works, both verse and prose, were first printed there. Milton, Thomas Browne, and many others, had their works printed at Amsterdam and Leyden, sometimes in Dutch as well as in English versions. It is the period of the pocket classics produced by the Elzevir Press, while many of our best surviving quartos and folios of the period were published by Janssen, Blaeu or Plantin at Amsterdam, Leyden and Utrecht. The pre-eminence of Amsterdam in printing and book-selling was itself largely the result of her geographical and economic position. Daniel Defoe, almost as good an economist as he was a novelist, wrote of the Dutch that they were :

"The Middle Persons in Trade, the factors and brokers of Europe : —they *buy* to *sell* again, *take* in to *send* out : and the greatest part of their vast commerce consists in being supply'd from All Parts of the world, that they may supply All the World again."

Fortunately in some ways, unfortunately in others, Defoe's description of the character of the economic functions of the Dutch was almost as accurate an account of the state of their culture, which by 1700 had lost much of its originality and vitality largely by reason of the continual traffic in foreign ideas and fashions. Even while Holland was at war with France, the Dutch intelligentsia showed itself as anxious to absorb or affect French literary fashions as the gallants of Dutch society were to ape, in ludicrous detail, the mannerisms of Versailles. As a counterweight to this, the later passion for things English could hardly fail to be salutary.

What had England to offer ? She had, of course the poets and drama-tists of the Elizabethan, Jacobean and Restoration periods ; she had Milton and the Metaphysicals. These were known and admired in Holland. But on the whole prose was more to the Dutchman's taste than poetry, and philosophy more popular than the drama. (Burney in his *Memoirs of European Music* (1773) tells us that Amsterdam had no theatre save for an occasional booth set up by travelling actors at the fair.) The philosophy

61

of Shaftesbury and Locke was much to the Dutch taste, and was no doubt given a topical flavour by the memory of those authors' residence in Holland. But above all, the Dutch admired English "social" literature— the journals and broadsheets of London's coffee-houses and literary claques. This literary life was itself symbolic of an important social change in England, where literature, philosophy and decent manners were ceasing to be the exclusive property of a small minority of educated people. The champions of taste and respectability were drawing together—from the merchants and bankers of the City, from the Universities and even the Church and the Sects : the London of Johnson's day (which he maintained was the most civilised city in the world) was in the process of forming. There was something like a conscious effort to achieve standards of taste and conduct, to uproot the boorishness that lingered in rural corners and visited London in season, to put to shame the sensuality flaunted at the Court and in society, to exterminate the drunkenness and dirt that festered in Gin Alley : in short, to try and make a world fit for the respectable brewers and bankers who were to be the patrons of Johnson, Garrick and Reynolds. As yet the attack on society was directed by the satirist rather than the preacher. Society had had its bellyful of restoration pleasure, but there were still enough people alive who remembered stories of the Major-Generals to fight shy of correction from the pulpit. Until the time of Whitefield and Wesley, the way of salvation was not to be made too narrow. Philosophers exalted the classical virtues, the coffee-houses buzzed with the astringent malice of wit against wit, and even the theatre entered upon a period of classical moderation, looking forward to the day when the actress, her ambition no longer limited to the dubious honour of becoming the mistress of the rake or the gallant, might aspire to be the companion of the philosopher and the artist. The chief missionary in this campaign to refine and civilize society was the *Spectator*, which said of itself that it "brought philosophy out of the closets and libraries, schools and colleges to dwell in clubs and Assemblies, at Tea Tables and in Coffee Houses."

The *Spectator* evoked a response in Holland which far exceeded anything enjoyed by other forms of writing. That the growth of a bourgeoisie with a thirst for taste and elegance had something to do with its vogue is undoubted ; but by comparison with the mood of English society there was this difference. The literary response to the spread of wealth was slower and less spontaneous in Holland. The age of Hooft and Vondel was the heroic age of Dutch literature. With the peak of Dutch commercial prosperity there had come a decline of literary genius and a mania for the superficialities of French style and manners which produced no native writing of any merit and threatened to stifle what local talent still remained. A reaction was inevitable, and it came in the person of Justus van Effen, of Utrecht. Van Effen was educated at Utrecht University, and first came to England in 1715 as an Under Secretary at the Embassy. In

HOLLANDSCHE
SPECTATOR,
DOOR
Mr. *JUSTUS van EFFEN*,
LID VAN DE KONINKLYKE MAATSCHAPPYE
DER WETENSCHAPPEN TE LONDEN.

TWEEDE DRUK

Vermeerderd met het LEVEN van den Schry-
ver en een Nieuw breedvoerig REGISTER
over het geheele Werk.

EERSTE DEEL.

Te *AMSTERDAM*,
By K. VAN TONGERLO EN F. HOUTTUIN. 1756,

THE DUTCH *SPECTATOR*
Engraved title-page to a revised edition, 1756

the same year he was made a member of the Royal Society and met Newton,
Pope and Swift. Later he returned to Holland and worked at Leyden
University. In 1727 he came back to England as Secretary to an old pupil
who represented Holland at the coronation of George II—an event which
van Effen celebrated in verse. The early papers for which van Effen
was largely responsible—the *Misantrope* and the *Bagatelle*—were written
in French, although they bear the mark of his stay in England ; and he
was already borrowing from Addison and Steele. Like them, van Effen
attacked what he considered were the worst of the current vices—de-
bauchery, duelling, atheism and ignorance—and exalted education and the

social virtues. By the time he came to write the *Hollandsche Spectator*, his ideas had crystallised and his heart had hardened against those French influences by which even his own work and style had been affected. For one thing, he wrote quite deliberately in his own language in defiance of polite convention. Nevertheless, it is symptomatic of the dilemma of his countrymen, caught as they were in the prevailing European cross-currents, that van Effen, in order to eject the French devil, had to introduce the English—though in this instance it fortunately transpired that the last state was not worse than the first. Van Effen kept his eye steadily on his ultimate object—to purge Dutch society of French fopperies and affectations which threatened to make the educated Dutchman look absurd, to encourage his countrymen in a confidence in themselves and their own native culture, and to shape a Dutch prose style comparable with the flowing measure of his English models.

The *Hollandsche Spectator*, which ran from August 20th 1731, to April 8th 1735, was modelled very closely on its English namesake, as van Effen acknowledged frankly in the first number. "The English work which I propose not to translate but to imitate in my mother toungue . . ."

For the most part, he tilted at the same sort of victim as Addison and Steele ; for society in Holland had not changed much since the seventeenth century, and the scenes that inspired Jan Steen provoked van Effen in much the same way as the London of Hogarth provoked Addison. Yet there was a difference. It was Owen Feltham who had described the Dutch "drinking down the Evening Starre and drinking up the Morning Starre." The idea became popular, and Sir Thomas Overbury repeated the charge : "Concerning the people : they are neither much devout, nor much wicked ; given all to drink, and eminently to no other vice : hard in bargaining, but just ; surly and respectless, as in all democracies ; thirsty, industrious and cleanly——" and so on. Amsterdam may have had, it seems, more grossness but less vice than London. There was, however, one important change since the riper, lustier days of Tromp and de Ruyter, Jan Steen and Ostade ; the Netherlands had been overrun by French manners and fopperies, which threatened to destroy her independence and sap her spirit—or so it seemed to van Effen ; and he is seen at his best in a paper like the *Ware en Valsche Beschaving* (*True and False Politeness*) in which he ridicules the scented, powdered society of the day which knew no conversation except the exchange of fatuous, empty compliments, when even the independent Dutchman had become afraid to speak his mind lest he be condemned as a boor by the standards of Versailles. Rather (I feel he might have said) let us have the surly, respectless, hard-drinking democracy of Overbury. But not quite : there was a middle way between extremes : kindliness and good-nature were not wholly extinct nor were they the monopoly of any one class or nation. Then let each individual, each order of society and each nation be true to its own nature, without trying to give the peat-cutter the airs of the courtier or the Dutchman

FLOWERS, STRAWBERRIES AND INSECTS
Oil painting by Jacob Walscappelle, fl. 1667-1717

By courtesy of Mr. Eugene Slat

PEWTER, SILVER AND GLASS
Oil painting by Pieter Claesz, 1641

the graces of the Parisian dandy. To this extent it was the satirist's acid rather than the reformer's zeal that was called for, and two remedies were ready to hand—the practical philosophy of Locke and the wisdom of Addison—"the English Socrates." If Effen's wit is less brilliant than Addison's in his journal, it has other solid qualities of its own, and for all his close imitation of the English model, van Effen manages to infuse something typically Dutch into his papers. Although no successor appeared immediately to whom he could hand his task, he achieved a great deal towards making a mercantile society, absorbed in the increasingly difficult business of making a national living, conscious of its short-comings, and towards creating a taste for good literature in Holland. Above all, he succeeded in reviving his countrymen's interest in the pos-sibilities of their own language, largely by observing and following the examples of his English contemporaries—the bite and thrust of Swift, the easy simplicity of Addison, the colloquialism of Defoe—by using Dutch words where he could, and by avoiding Gallicisms. If contemporary Dutch prose was forced and stiff, that was not a fault inherent in the language but the shortcomings of the writers' wit and imagination. Van Effen set out quite deliberately to eliminate those faults :

"Since my aim is to bring entertainment and profit to all my fellow citizens, I will apply myself specially to considerations of intelligibility and perspicuity . . . Although I shall endeavour to flex my expressions to the matter, I will throughout strive to avail myself of the familiar style such as has been established by usage among people of birth and education. . . . I will watch for long extended periods, in which it is the custom, after the Latin, to bring up the verb, upon which the whole sentence depends, at the end . . . Also I will, for the sake of clarity, carefully eschew those long parentheses . . . which is some of our writers, enclose and again enclose within themselves other parentheses like nest-boxes and necessarily produce confusion in the mind of the reader." (From W. J. Pienaar's *English Influences in Dutch Literature and Justus van Effen as Intermediary. Cambridge* 1929.)

Addison, then, is van Effen's hero and chief model, but he introduces many other authors to his readers—Shakespeare, Milton, Spenser, Swift (whose *Tale of a Tub* he translated) Sidney, Pope, Defoe (he translated *Robinson Crusoe*), Mandeville, Shaftesbury, as well as the philosophy of Locke and the scientific writings of Newton. Van Effen did not, however, accept everything English with the indiscriminate enthusiasm which his opponents extended to everything French. It is true that he once de-scribed the English as "one of the wisest and most reasonable Nations on the face of the earth" but it is only fair to add that he could on occasion be severely critical. The English press, for example, he condemned as irresponsible and licentious.

After the *Hollandsche Spectator*, the paper which did most to make English writing known in the Netherlands was the *Boekzaal* of William

Sewell, a Dutchman of English descent, who carried on van Effen's work of spreading English ideas in philosophy, theology and natural science. Once firmly planted, the love and appreciation of English literature did not die easily in the Netherlands. The works of Laurence Sterne became tremendously popular. "Sterne Clubs" became the rage, and a period of something very like Anglomania ensued. The novels of Richardson in particular appealed to Dutch readers, and their popularity is reflected in the romances of Betje Wolf and Aagje Deken. Jacob van Lennep in his historical novels modelled himself closely on Scott, while the writings of Nicholas Beets were strongly influenced by Sterne, Scott, Byron and (later in life) by Dickens. Amongst the poets of the nineteenth century, Jacques Perk was inspired by the works of Keats and Shelley.

The debt which Dutch literature owes to English models is a considerable one. But there was a contra-account. While the Dutch borrowed, they also broadcast. To assess the effects of the continuous diffusion of English ideas by Dutch writers, translators, printers and booksellers would mean much laborious research but it would be a worthwhile appendix to the history of the struggle for a free press in seventeenth and eighteenth century England. It would show, I think, that in the age of the Licensing Acts and the libel laws—an age by the way when English printing was technically and artistically at its worst—the presses of Amsterdam, Leyden and Utrecht offered a providential alternative medium of expression, printing for the Royalists when the Parliament men controlled the licensing system and giving voice to the opposition to the Licenser of the Press when that office was revived by Charles II. In Holland the effects of this intercourse were not limited to the infusion into the Dutch vocabulary of a hundred English words and phrases. The works of English authors took a firm hold on the affections of the reading public, enjoying an extraordinary popularity which lasted into the days of Shaw, Priestley, Wells and Edgar Wallace. In the eighteenth century, the packet sailing between London and Rotterdam or from Harwich to Helvoetsluys carried a steady flow of English books and newspapers to Holland. Thence, stowed in with bales of broadcloth from Devon, and barrels of spices from the Indies, they found their way to France, Germany, Italy and to all Europe. Similarly the translations and editions from Plantin and the pocket-classics from Elzevirs found their way from Amsterdam and Leyden to Paris and Potsdam, Genoa, St. Petersburg and London. It was part of the elusive process by which England was brought back into the main stream of the European tradition after the upheavals of the seventeenth century which threatened her with backward provincialism. Macaulay once wrote "France has been the interpreter between England and mankind." That is to leave out a link—the link which the Dutch men of letters and Dutch printers formed between England and France. They gave France not merely the science of Newton and the philosophy of Locke but by a constant process of diffusion a whole range of the best in English literature.

ARTIST SKETCHING
Pen and wash drawing by Rembrandt van Rijn, 1606-1669

PAINTING, ARCHITECTURE AND DESIGN

It is a commonplace of political history that military invasions have often been preceded by what has been called economic penetration. The landing at Torbay in 1688 was no exception, as I have tried to show elsewhere in this book. There were Dutch merchants in London, Kings Lynn and Exeter, Dutch and Flemish weavers in East Anglia, Dutch engineers by the Humber and the Ouse, in the Isle of Ely and the Isle of Thanet. But there was also another kind of penetration—and having succumbed to jargon we may as well persevere in it—what we may call the artistic penetration. If it has been less advertised than the influences which radiated from Versailles or from Florence, that is perhaps because there are so many affinities between England and Holland that the fusion of ideas was less perceptible, gentler, more subtle than the spectacular impact of a Latin upon an Anglo-Saxon civilisation which produced the Italianate Englishman of the sixteenth century or his descendant of the Restoration. Nevertheless, it was a Fleming—van Dyck—and a Dutchman —Peter Lely—who founded the English school of portrait painting : but long before van Dyck was appointed to the Court, there were Flemish and Dutch artists working in England : and long after the Golden Age had passed away in Holland, the influence of the Dutch genius remained strong amongst English painters. As one might expect, it was the artists from those parts of England which had most affinities with Holland—

RIVER SCENE WITH BOATS
Oil painting by Jan van Goyen, 1646

East Anglia—who remained most susceptible to the spell of Hobbema
and van de Capelle. To them, the North Sea was not so much a barrier
as a highway linking two worlds which had much in common.

Curiously enough, the two centuries which produced some of the
greatest of English poetry, prose, drama and music, showed little spon-
taneity in art. Even the frequent and disastrous incidence of war and
religious upheaval can hardly account for the absence of great painting in
Tudor England. The lavish patronage of the Stuart courts, and the grow-
ing demand for portrait painting, only served to emphasise the strange
lack of native talent. Daniel Mytens, Paul van Somer, Cornelius Johnson,
Gerard Soest, Marc Gheeraerdts, Pieter Borsseler, Abraham van Diepen-
beke, the van de Veldes, Peter Lely—these are the names which go to
make up the "English" school of seventeenth century painters. Yet they
are all Flemish or Dutch artists who were attracted to England by the
promise of handsome patronage between 1600 and 1680. Over them all
towers the figure of van Dyck, who settled in London as Court painter
in 1632 and who was to dominate English portrait painting for a century
and a half. Even before his arrival, there were already two Netherlands
painters of some stature working in England. The first, Daniel Mytens,
was a Dutch pupil of Rubens, who was appointed Court painter to James I.
Mytens was a gifted painter whose work ranges between the literalness of
his Dutch contemporaries and the fuller magnificence of van Dyck ; his
portrait of Charles I is in the first manner, his *James, Second Marquess
of Hamilton* in the second. Cornelius Johnson, the son of a Fleming, was
born in London, and during his English period his work has a good deal
in common with van Dyck's. Both Mytens and Johnson returned to
Holland in later years, conscious, no doubt, that they were being over-
shadowed by the genius of van Dyck and Lely. With the appointment of

68

THE MILKMAID
Oil painting by Jan Vermeer, 1632-1675.

van Dyck to the Court in 1632, a new era opened in English painting. I say "English" advisedly because no one has ever infused into the painting of English men and women the character of an age and society as did the Netherlander van Dyck. Or was it the other way round—was it van Dyck's genius which helped to create the Cavalier legend? It is interesting to speculate how our conception of the Stuart age has been shaped by van Dyck and his Dutch successor, Lely, as well as by that attractive impostor of Hals "The Laughing Cavalier" who presumably owes his English reputation to a not unreasonable English conviction that Dutch artists only painted Englishmen. For no Englishman appeared to immortalise the Cavalier except William Dobson, and he too was a pupil of van Dyck.

69

Even Robert Walker, the Puritan painter of Puritans, of Cromwell and Hampden, followed the van Dyck manner.

The later years of the Republican period and the Restoration are dominated by another Dutch artist, Sir Peter Lely, a pupil of de Grebber of Haarlem, who came over in 1641 in the train of William, Prince of Orange ; the occasion was William's marriage to Charles I's daughter Mary, and Lely's portraits of the bridal couple helped to establish his reputation here, bringing him an extensive clientele. Lely, (with a facility odd in a Dutchman) quickly adapted himself to the van Dyck tradition —so much so that some of his portraits have been ascribed to van Dyck or his pupils. His best known works are comprised in the *Flagmen* collection in the Maritime Museum at Greenwich, and in the *Windsor Beauties* at Hampton Court. The latter—especially the portraits of Lady Byrom and Lady Falmouth—have been held to set Lely apart as a colourist and portrait painter. Yet as a collection *The Beauties* fall short of the uniform perfection of the *Flagmen* portraits. In his diary for 18th April 1666, Pepys writes—

"To Mr. Lilly's, the painters, and there saw the heads—some finished and all begun—of the flagg-men in the late great fight with the Duke of York against the Dutch. The Duke of York hath them done to hang in his Chamber, and very finely they are done indeed. Here are the Prince's [Rupert's], Sir George Askue's, Sir Thomas Teddiman's, Sir Christopher Ming's, Sir Joseph Jorden, Sir William Berkeley, Sir Thomas Allen, and Captain Harman's, as also the Duke of Albermarle's ; and will be my Lord Sandwich's, Sir W. Penn's and Sir Jeremy Smith's."

If it is strange that we should owe our conception of the English Cavalier partly to a Fleming, it is no less curious that the finest portrait of a seventeenth century English Admiral—the portrait of the dour Sir Jeremy Smith on which the paint was not yet dry when Pepys saw it—should have been painted by a Dutchman. Yet it was typical of the age that neither sitter nor artist should have felt any embarrassment on the political count. Perhaps it was his Dutch training that enabled Lely to adapt himself to the sombre mood of the *Flagmen* more easily than to the contemporary tastes of the Court in female beauty. Many fine examples of Lely's genius other than those in the two main collections are extant—none better than the excellent portrait of Tobias Rustat, Treasurer to Charles II, which hangs in the Hall of Jesus College, Cambridge.

Gerard Soest, the painter of the famous *Aubrey de Vere, Earl of Oxford* (in the Dulwich Gallery) was another Dutchman who came to England about the same time as Lely : if not a pupil of Lely's, his work is certainly in the van Dyck-Lely tradition. A later (and lesser) arrival, Jacob Huysmans, the Antwerper, enjoyed a considerable reputation for a time, and was considered by some "to exceed Lilly."

By 1680, when Lely died, a few English artists were beginning to appear—notably John Riley, a pupil of Soest and later of Lely, and John

ADMIRAL SIR JEREMIAH SMITH
Oil painting by Sir Peter Lely, 1618-1680

Greenhill. But the greatest figure was still that of the foreigner—a German
it is true, but Dutch by training and tradition. Sir Godfrey Kneller studied
in Holland, apparently with the great Ferdinand Bol. With Kneller we
come to the establishment of a school of English portrait painting, and .
the Dutch names become fewer.

Van Dyck, Lely, Mytens, Soest—these are the greatest names, but
there were many other lesser men who worked in England—Adrian
Hanneman of the Hague, Abraham Hondius of Rotterdam, and Isaak
Luttichuys of Amsterdam and many more. The portrait painters were not the
only artists to be attracted by the generous royal and aristocratic patronage
which England offered. The painters of seascapes and landscapes were
also well represented. Of the former, the greatest were undoubtedly the

71

van de Veldes, appointed to the Court by the special charter of Charles II in 1676, who rivalled the greatness of Lely's admirals in their paintings of sea scenes and naval battles and their *grisaille* drawings of ships. Amongst the landscape painters we might mention Josse de Momper, David Vinckenboon, Francis Cleyn, and Thomas Wyck, who specialised in views of London.

With the eighteenth century came a rapid decline in the quality of art in the Netherlands, a decline that was reflected in a reduction in the number of Dutch artists working in England. A handful of painters and sculptors (like Scheemakers, Rysbrach and van Nost) was still to be found, but the time of Dutch preponderance was over. The influence of the Netherlands school, however, was undiminished. Van Dyck and Lely remained the giants of the world of portraiture ; even the truculent Hogarth, though he affected to despise the imitators of foreign fashions, learnt much from the brutal realism of Jan Steen and Ostade. But perhaps the most remarkable development was the gradual unfolding in the eastern counties of a style of landscape painting which owed at any rate its beginnings to the study of the Dutch Masters—of Cuyp, Hobbema, and Ruysdael. The artists of East Anglia shared with these a flat or gently undulating landscape that did not lend itself to heroics : this—the "dull" country—was the home of most of the best English landscape painters while more dramatic scenery has only gladdened a thousand Victorian back-parlours with *The Highland Glen* and *A Stag at Bay*. The native scene of Gainsborough, Crome and Constable was a land of windmills, locks and waterways, creeks and inlets and sea views. Not only the homely and pastoral subjects, but conditions

MOONRISE ON THE MARSHES OF THE YARE
Oil painting by John Crome, 1768-1821

of atmosphere and light were very similar in both countries. That permanent April state (which the meteorologists have immortalised as "bright intervals"), a state in which darkening clouds for ever threaten a fugitive sunshine, was nature's gift to a race of artists whose genius lay above all in the study of light. The early landscapes of Gainsborough (a Suffolk man) were strongly influenced by the works of Jan Wynants and other minor Dutch artists whose pictures were frequently to be found in private collections in East Anglian houses. John Constable, another East Anglian, was (as his pictures so often remind us) the son of a miller who owned both windmills and watermills. It was John Crome, however, who symbolized most vividly the closeness of eastern England to Holland, and yet at the same time managed to achieve a sense of local and purely English atmosphere which bears comparison with the achievements of Hobbema, Ruysdael or the Vermeer of the *View of Delft*. Whether it is the windmill and sails of his *Moonrise on the Yare* (reminiscent of van de Neer) or the ships in his *Yarmouth Harbour* (which owed much to Albert Cuyp) or the tawny sails of his last picture *Yarmouth Water Frolic*, here

73

is an artist who was intimately linked not only in technique but in temper with the great Dutch masters of the seventeenth century. One cannot help wondering whether John Crome had any connections with the Dutch colonies of Norwich or Colchester, or at any rate whether it was perhaps through some of the wealthier of the Dutch settlers that the Eastern Counties were introduced to Dutch art. There is evidence of the same influence though in a lesser degree in other artists—in Cotman, Bonington and even Turner. In every case, however, the Dutch tradition was absorbed and adapted into a new, and unmistakably English, synthesis. Nowhere was there mere slavish imitation, though occasionally the literalness which suited a Hobbema or a Ruysdael became a handicap to lesser men. On the whole, the Dutch model was what a model should be—a stimulus to be like but different : allowing a wide scope for local variation yet withal near enough in subject and in temper to provide an attainable ideal. Paradoxically enough the example of Hobbema and Cuyp, and to a lesser degree of Ruysdael, was an indispensable element in the formation of an original and characteristically English School of landscape painting in the eighteenth century : but all the time, the English painters were moving away from realism to impressionism. Crome—Constable—Turner each represents a step in a typically English process of assimilation and

MILKMAID AND COWS NEAR DORDRECHT
Oil painting by Albert Cuyp, 1620-1691

74

SKITTLE PLAYERS
Oil painting by Jan Steen, c. 1652

change. Here, long after the great Dutchmen had gone, the Dutch genius lived on in new forms : the story goes that Gainsborough died as he had lived speaking of van Dyck and tradition has it that John Crome died with Hobbema's name on his lips.

Flemish and Dutch influences were hardly less pronounced in architecture than in painting during the last decade of the sixteenth and the first half of the seventeenth century. In East Anglia especially,

CUSTOMS HOUSE, KINGS LYNN, NORFOLK
Water colour by Mona Moore, 1941

the stepped and curled gables (introduced first possibly by the immigrant weavers from the Low Countries in their own houses and cottages) became a native style ; the Hall at Fen Ditton, the cottages at Fen Stanton and Fen Drayton, the 'White Hart' at Scole, and the Fishermen's Almshouses at Yarmouth are only a few examples out of hundreds. That the fashion was not so lasting in its architectural as in its artistic phase is due to the fact that while the painters of the Northern Netherlands were emancipating themselves from Italian influences in this period, the architects, there as in England, were falling more and more under classical influences.

In fact, one of the valuable contributions made by the Dutch architects and writers of text-books of this period was to transmit to us scale-drawings of the designs of the Italian masters—of Serlio, Vignola and Palladio. The result was that while the Dutch style in painting was becoming more and more characteristic, Dutch architecture was steadily absorbing more Southern influences as time went on, and indeed is often merged and lost in the comprehensive term "Palladianism." In fact, Dutch architecture retained several important distinctive features which were

76

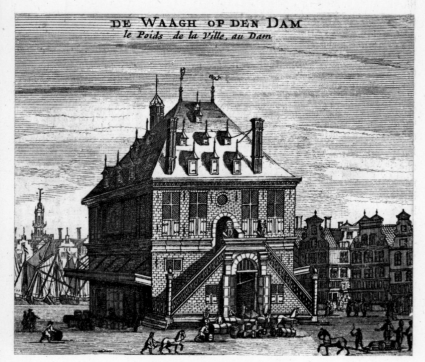

DE WAAGH OP DEN DAM
le Poids de la Ville, au Dam

OLD WEIGH-HOUSE, AMSTERDAM
Engraving, 1693

taken over by the English architects of the late seventeenth and early eighteenth centuries, and embodied in the Georgian style.

Some of the architects who did much to popularise Netherlandish fashions in English design were themselves Flemish or Dutch; others were Englishmen who had learned from Dutch craftsmen or Dutch textbooks. Amongst the immigrant designers were Casper Vosbergh, who worked for Cecil at Burghley House, Stamford; Henry de Pas, who is credited with the design of Sir Thomas Gresham's Exchange (Gresham's own life-story is symbolic of the close economic relations existing between the two countries in Tudor times, when, as often later, the sinews of England's war potential were formed over the sea); and Bernard Jansen, who was largely responsible for Audley End. More shadowy but not less interesting, was "the ingenious and learned Captain Wynne (or Winde)" a native of Bergen-op-Zoom, the designer of Hamstead Marshall (now destroyed), Newcastle House, Lincoln's Inn Fields, and old Buckingham House. (Wynne's original drawings for Hamstead Marshall are still in the Bodleian). The continual flow of craftsmen and ideas from the Netherlands reached its climax in the early seventeenth century, the period when

Dutch ideas—curled gables and scrolls, strapwork and the extensive use of brickwork—were at the height of their popularity. Especially during the middle years of Charles I's reign, the number of houses, town residences as well as country mansions, in the "Dutch Gable" style, multiplied. Raynham Hall, Norfolk, with its smooth brickwork, stone quoins and dressings, is a typical and magnificent example. Others like Broome Park, Kent (1635) and Swakeleys, Middlesex, (1638) had wooden mullions. Lilford Hall, Northamptonshire, belongs to the same period and style, as does Ashdown House, Berkshire, (built by John Webb, nephew and pupil of Inigo Jones, for the first Lord Craven) which still towers over the Berkshire Downs. Amsterdam House, at Christchurch, Hampshire, built of bricks specially imported from the Netherlands, was unfortunately pulled down some years ago. In London itself, there was a number of houses in the Dutch style, one of the finest surviving examples being the house we to-day call Kew Palace. The original house on the site was bought in 1630 from a Dutch merchant by another Dutchman, Samuel Fortrey, who pulled it down and built the present house in the following year. Kew Palace has most of the usual features of the Dutch style—the carved gables and fine brickwork in Flemish bond—and both the Palace and the nearby cottage (also in the same style) are enhanced by their magnificent setting. In this they are more fortunate than Schomberg House in Pall Mall, an example of the later Dutch style, classical in mood but still showing a good deal of Dutch influence in the elevation, which was built for the Duke in 1698.

Interior design reflects the same trend; elaborate and sometimes hideous chimney pieces were copied from Flemish examples, of which a good specimen may be found at Knole, Kent. The popularity of Delft

A LADY AND GENTLEMAN
English tiles of enamelled earthenware. Eighteenth century

ADAM AND EVE : THE FLOOD : THE GOLDEN CALF : JACOB AND RACHEL
Dutch tiles of enamelled earthenware.   Eighteenth century

tiles has been touched on elsewhere but one interesting example may be
worth quoting. When Marlborough House was being built, Wren wrote
to Sarah to say that 12,000 Dutch tiles would be needed for the rooms,
and about 2,200 for the chimneys. (October 31st 1710.) Possibly Marlborough may have turned a returning supply ship to good account to
meet the occasion. At the Queen's House, Greenwich, blue and white
Delft tiles formed a dado in one of the rooms.

What of the furniture? The period which lies between the Glorious
Revolution and, say, 1747 (when the tax on mahogany was lifted) is the
age of walnut in England : it is moreover, the time when English conceptions of domestic comfort and convenience underwent a rapid change.
A typical house of 1690 or 1700 would contain many pieces of furniture
previously unknown in England—china cabinets for the new Delft or
oriental wares, mirrors in veneered frames surrounded by floral designs
in rich marquetry in the manner of van Huysum, a long-case clock
veneered with marquetry, writing cabinets, washstands and tallboys, and

TENDING TULIPS IN THE STADTSTUIN, AMSTERDAM
Engraving, 1614

lacquered furniture in imitation of the Chinese work imported by the Dutch East India Company. There would probably be a suite of furniture, designed by Daniel Marot, the Huguenot refugee who came over in the service of William and Mary and the greatest of the foreign craftsmen working in England (if we exclude Grinling Gibbons). There would be chairs richly upholstered in velvet or in tapestry worked by the Flemings of Mortlake, who were induced to settle there by James I and survived throughout the walnut period. Most of these fashions in walnut were borrowed from the Dutch designers and cabinet makers, who in turn borrowed from so many other sources—French, Spanish and Oriental—that to identify and distinguish is often difficult if not impossible. Meanwhile, the English craftsman was rapidly becoming proficient in these imported fashions and was soon successfully cutting and laying veneers with and without marquetry, and imitating the lacquered magnificence of his foreign rival. He learnt, too, new methods of construction from the Dutch craftsmen. Screws and lapped dovetail joints replaced the Birmingham nail that had served well enough for the old days of oak but was necessarily ousted from the new and more refined world of highly-polished and figured surfaces : he learnt to cut his timber at such an angle as to obtain the richest effects from the tones and lines of the grain : even knots and burrs were cut so as to provide patterned veneers of the greatest beauty. Above all, he learned to turn a cabriole leg—probably a form of ancient oriental origin—which began its long period of popularity about this time. In short it was during these years, with their astonishing and sometimes garish variety of styles, that the English craftsman learned to assimilate many of the methods and designs which were later incorporated in the work of his great successors in the age of Chippendale, Hepplewhite and Sheraton.

In the same period, the Dutch garden, with its high, thick, clipped yew hedges and box trees curling into fantastic shapes—heraldic beasts, ships and even Biblical tableaux—became so fashionable that it was in the end killed by its own ludicrous extravagance. The geometrical precision of the Dutch style did not, it must be confessed, really fit the English scene, and the visitor to Levens Hall, Westmorland, will probably sympathise with the *Spectator* when he writes :

"Our trees rise in Cones, Globes and Pyramids. We see the Marks of the Scissors upon every Plant and Bush. I do not know whether I am singular in my opinion, but, for my own part, I would rather look upon a Tree in all its Luxuriancy and Diffusion of Boughs and Branches than when it is thus cut and trimmed into a Mathematical Figure."

Our 'Cabbage' rose (or Batavian rose as it was called) seems to have been almost extinct in W. Europe in the Middle Ages. It reappears in the Netherlands in the last quarter of the sixteenth century when it is

PRUNING TREES
Detail from Meindert Hobbema's 'Avenue Middelharnis', 1689

BURDOCK
Oil painting by John Crome, 1768-1821

commented on by the great Dutch botanist Clusius. Apparently it was not commonly grown until the second quarter of the next century : as its popularity grew we find it appearing occasionally in the paintings of Justus van Huysum, and regularly and indubitably in those of his son

STILL-LIFE
Oil painting by Jan van Huysum, 1682-1749

Jan van Huysum, the greatest of the Dutch flower painters. Where it
came from, it is hard to say : possibly it was brought back from the Levant
by one of the many Dutch traders there. At any rate, it is certainly from
the Netherlands that it was introduced into England and France.

WREN STEEPLE
St. Bride's, London

The pattern of the formal Dutch style, with its coloured gravels and its brass and lead statues, was nicely calculated to eke out the limited plots behind the great houses by the canals of the Dutch towns: imposed on the spacious and natural beauty of English park land, it was apt to become a horticultural strait-jacket. Perhaps the best examples of the Dutch style are Wrest Park (Bedfordshire), Melbourne (Derbyshire) —both adorned with van Nost's work— and Hampton Court.

The popularity of the Dutch style in architecture, at any rate in its most obvious and characteristic form as at Kew Palace or Raynham, was shortlived. Other styles, chiefly Italian and French, soon toned down its native originality and we must look closely to discern its continuing influence in more subtle forms in the work of Christopher Wren and his followers. It has often been remarked upon as a rather curious fact that Wren travelled abroad very little. A partial explanation may be that Wren had upon his shelves a number of folios into which contemporary Dutch writers on architecture had concentrated the essentials of Renascence design and experience. We know that some of these were available to Wren, and we know that in 1641 his friend John Evelyn, the diarist, visited the Amsterdam shop of Hondius and Blaeu, buying books and maps of Serlio and Vignola. Serlio's *Bookes of Architecture* were first translated from Italian into Dutch and later, in 1611, from Dutch into English.

In 1631 Cornelius Danckert published his *Architectura Moderna* containing many of Hendrik de Keyser's works at Amsterdam. Bloem's *Boek van de Vijf Columnen van Architecture*, which was already in existence, was in Evelyn's collection.

84

Hendrik Hondius's own *Les Cinq Rangs de L'Architecture* had appeared in Amsterdam in 1617. All these books contained scale drawings and were most probably known to Wren.

Perhaps the most influential of all, however, were the works of Philip Vingboon. His designs for town houses of the kind which may still be seen along the canals of Amsterdam, such as the great house built for Trips, the bankers, in 1662, undoubtedly influenced Wren and helped to bring to maturity the style we call the Georgian Vernacular, and which we think of as perhaps the most typically English of architectural styles. At the same time the designs of Jacob van Campen, the architect of the Royal Palace at Amsterdam, in the manner of Palladio and Scamozzi, were being published. Other ideas which Wren probably

AMSTERDAM GATE TOWERS
From C. Danckert's *Architectura Moderna*, 1631

borrowed from Holland were the sash window (which was well-known there early in the century) and the combination of broad surfaces of brick with stone quoins. These borrowings were not limited to domestic architecture. Medieval English church building could show no precedent for the Wren steeples, with their mounting stages of concave and convex ornament, but they have their antecedents in earlier Dutch spires such as the Zuiderkerk and the Westertoren at Amsterdam. It seems reasonable to suppose that Wren assimilated at least some of these ideas from the designs of Danckert and Hondius for it was a mark of his greatness that he was able to draw on the experience of others and make of it something especially suited to the English scene, the English temperament and the English climate. By 1688 Wren had helped to fuse some of the best elements of Dutch and English design. Thereafter, the lines of architectural development in England and Holland were to run very nearly parallel.

FACTORY FOR SILK WEAVING
Trade card, eighteenth century

SCOTLAND AND HOLLAND 1600-1800

Trade was the link which bound Holland to many countries during the seventeenth century, and there were few ports of any size in Europe where the trim, squat ships from Rotterdam and Amsterdam were not a familiar sight. But with Scotland the Dutch had very special bonds. Scottish sheep from the Southern Uplands supplied a large part of the wool upon which the Netherlands cloth-making industry depended, and Middelburg and Veere had competed long and bitterly for the privilege of monopolising this lucrative trade. After years of wrangling and quarrelling and a score of indeterminate law-suits, the trade was eventually allocated to Veere during the sixteenth century, and there the Scottish staple flourished for two centuries, only dwindling into obscurity and decay when the Leyden cloth industry itself declined, and finally disappearing with the Revolutionary Wars. At Veere in peacetime, you could still see what E. V. Lucas called "the beautifully grave" *Schotsche Huis* on the quay, once the headquarters of the flourishing wool trade, and now a museum. This was the residence of the Scottish Conservators, the officials appointed by the King to govern the Staple. Amongst the seventeenth century Conservators are two curious figures who deserve mention—Thomas Cunningham, who supplied the Covenanting armies of the Scottish Parliamentarians with arms and munitions on Dutch credit, and Sir William Davidson—merchant, speculator, spy, amateur theologian and gun-runner—who followed Cunningham as Conservator from 1662 to 1671.

86

But the ties which connected Scotland with Holland were stronger than those of mere commerce. In both countries Calvinism, with its emphasis on iron personal discipline and its rigid moral code for society, was the religion which appealed to men accustomed to wring a livelihood from a soil which grudged easy profits. In both lands the eternal problem of making bricks without straw moulded stern and uncompromising characters, and drove enterprising men abroad in search of riches. To these men, religion and theology were not dry or sterile enquiries. Medieval man had seen the hand of God intervening in the most mundane affairs : the conviction persisted amongst Calvinists long after it had been weakened by the growth of rationalism in more comfortable societies. The Scottish passion for theological disputation has become proverbial, but in the seventeenth century it paled beside a Puritan enthusiasm which pervaded the whole of Dutch society, of which a Jesuit remarked that everyone in the country from the chief rulers to the lowest yokel and sailor was thoroughly versed in the theology of Calvin. It is not surprising therefore to find that Scottish religion and learning, which were strongly under French influence in the sixteenth century, fall under the spell of Holland in the next. For while French Calvinism dwindled into sectarianism, Calvinism in Scotland and Holland rose militant, triumphant and intolerant. In Scotland, it became the creed of resistance to Royalist tyranny and to Popery, the creed for which the Covenanters fought and bled, while at Leyden and Haarlem, Dutchmen laid down their lives for their own way of life against the Spanish tyranny, and Calvinists sharpened their swords with bitter memories of the massacre at Naarden.

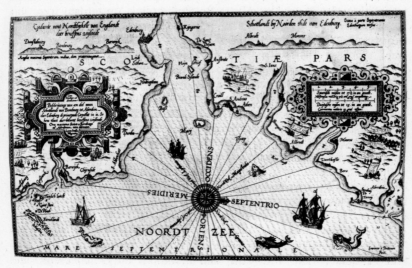

MAP OF THE FORTH ESTUARY
Engraving from Wagenaer's *Atlas*, 1588

87

It would, indeed, be difficult to overestimate the effect upon Scotland and upon Scottish religion of the Synod of Dort which sat at Dordrecht in 1619, or to exaggerate the veneration which later generations of Scotsmen accorded to its pronouncements. The Synod of Dort condemned, much to the delight of the Scottish Calvinists, the views of Jacobus Arminius, the Dutch theologian who had proclaimed the doctrine of free will in opposition to the orthodox Calvinist doctrine of predestination, and finally determined the shape of future orthodoxy in both Scotland and Holland. Henceforth, Arminianism to Scotland was to be identified with tyranny, illegal taxation, episcopacy, and even Popery. To Scotsmen, the Synod became known as "the famous Synod of Dort," "the renowned Synod," "the venerable Synod," etc., and its conclusions were used as a basis and test of orthodoxy for three centuries. Books, theses and sermons explaining and enlarging on its decisions were placed in the library at Glasgow College, and other Scottish University libraries can show similar collections of Dutch publications. The Westminster Assembly (1644-49), which determined religious standards for Scotland for later centuries, sat under its influence and inspiration. The most famous Scottish divines of the seventeenth century—John Forbes, Robert Baillie, John Menzies, Samuel Rutherford and many others—were strongly influenced by contemporary Dutch theologians both Predestinarian and Arminian, such as Voetius, Cocceijus, Hoornebeeck, Heinsius, Vossius, and even the great Grotius himself (though his religious views were in many ways more suited to a less bigoted age). John Forbes had himself been chaplain to the Company of Merchant Adventurers at Delft, and married a Dutch wife whom he took back to Aberdeen. Baillie had a cousin in Veere who sent him the latest Dutch theological works and kept him in touch with current discussions. Scottish theological works were often printed at Amsterdam, at this period the chief printing centre in Europe.

Meanwhile, the communities of Scottish traders and seamen in the principal Dutch cities and ports were settling down in an atmosphere which was politically and theologically congenial to them. At Amsterdam, the Church of the Begyns, an ancient Order of Nuns, standing in a little Court just off the Kalverstraat, was assigned to the Presbyterians in 1607. At Rotterdam, the States General and the Magistrates gave permission in 1642 for a Scottish Church to be instituted and even provided funds. After two removals, the Scottish Church was finally settled at the South end of the Schiedam (or Scottish Dyke, so called from its being inhabited by large numbers of Scotsmen), by the Leuvehaven, used from time immemorial by Scottish shipping. Along with the Church went a Scottish School and Poor House. At Campveere, the first Protestant clergyman was appointed in 1587. At Delft too, there was a wealthy and influential trading community: the Sessional Register of their Church begins in 1645. Dordrecht, which became a regular Scottish Staple port in 1668, supported a large Scottish population, and other communities were to be found at

IN A DUTCH COURTYARD
Oil painting by Pieter de Hooch, 1665

Flushing, Hertogenbosch, the Hague, Leyden, Middelburg and Utrecht. These groups of Scotsmen in Holland made up a varied society, comprising all sorts and conditions of men from poor sailors and fishermen to the wealthy merchants of Rotterdam and the titled aristocracy at the Hague, from peaceloving pastors like the virtuous Robert Fleming of Rotterdam to the grim fighters of the Scottish Brigade, who lived and fought as Scots for the House of Orange for more than two hundred years. This was the brigade which in 1578 sustained the brunt of the action at

Reminaut against the Spaniards, fighting "without armour and in their shirts." So much were they at home and so little interfered with that they were not naturalised until the American War. There was, at one time, at Zierikzee, a monument to a Henry Hume, an officer of the Brigade, described as a "Captain in the service of the United Netherlands," who died at Delft on May 28, 1650. This anonymous translation of the curious Dutch epitaph claims to retain "the spirit and quaintness of the original."

"When young I lost my Mother, but my loss I never knew,
For oh ! an aunt's maternal heart my filial homage drew.
Beneath her watchful care I sought whate'er adorns the mind,
In Sciences and arts, and tongues, and manners of mankind.
As Captain of our infantry, as horse-lieutenant too,
I shew'd unto my fatherland, a spirit bold and true.
And after God for two full years had made our battles cease,
He called me hence to spend with him the life of heavenly peace,
I do not grieve, because I die and part with wealth and state,
I only mourn, in that my aunt so sorely weeps my fate."

The reader is left to decide whether the gallant Captain's "fatherland" was Scotland or the Netherlands.

The ease with which these Scottish communities fitted into Dutch society contrasts strongly with the difficulties met with by most immigrant communities trading in foreign lands. No doubt both sides appreciated hard bargaining in business, but *odium theologicum*, the usual cause of friction, was entirely absent. There were no substantial differences between the systems of Church Government in the Dutch and Scottish Churches. Many Dutch names appear amongst the Deacons and Elders of the Scottish Churches in Holland, the Ministers of which (though usually Scottish) were members of the Dutch *Klassikaal-Bestuur* or *Classis*. Relations with the Dutch ecclesiastical authorities were cordial, save for an occasional brush with garrison chaplains who were apparently inclined to "conduct themselves in a violent manner." Nor did the Dutch language hold any terrors for the Scottish settlers and their pastors, many of whom became well-known as preachers and theological writers in the Dutch as well as their own language.

One consequence of these commercial ties and religious sympathies was that many Scotsmen went to the Netherlands to receive their University education. The process began with the pastors of the various Scottish trading communities and the chaplains to the Scottish troops serving in the Low Countries, who not infrequently attached themselves to the Dutch Universities. It was sustained by the flow of exiles, English and Scottish, who sought refuge in Holland from the religious persecutions and political violence of seventeenth century England and Scotland—men of such varied views and origin as John Robinson, pastor to the humble congregation of exiles at Leyden, the root from which the Pilgrim Fathers

THE MARKET PLACE, HAARLEM
Oil painting by G. A. Berckheyde, 1630-1698

sprang, and Charles Stuart, waiting and intriguing for his Restoration to
the throne of England. To all this oddly assorted company, the Universities of Leyden, Utrecht and Franeker offered refuge, hospitality and
prodigious learning. The trickle became a full stream, and hundreds of
students, some English but mainly Scottish, studied at these Universities
in the seventeenth and eighteenth centuries. Over eighty matriculated at
Leyden between 1620 and 1650. In 1700, it was said that one third of the
students at Leyden were English or Scottish, and during the eighteenth

century about 2,000 British students, a good proportion certainly Scots, matriculated at Leyden. Englishmen came there largely because of the lamentable state of the teaching at Oxford and Cambridge, and doubtless because of the educational disabilities imposed upon English dissenters at the English Universities. Scotsmen were attracted to Holland partly, as we have seen, because Dutch theology was congenial to them, partly because of their unpopularity at Oxford (Boswell, himself educated at Utrecht, bears witness to this) and partly because Utrecht gave a training in law invaluable to a Scotsman. Utrecht therefore usually contained a contingent of young Scottish aristocrats studying (nominally, at any rate) law against the day when they should assume their estates. For to be a successful landlord in Scotland, it was at least desirable to be a tolerable lawyer. Amongst these were the seond Earl of Marchmont and the third Earl of Argyll. But of the generations of Scottish and English students who passed through the Dutch Universities, from that ingenious English man, William Petty, who came back from Leyden with his head full of mathematics, statistics, map making and shipbuilding, to the mercurial and Irish Goldsmith, and the errant, melancholy and Scottish Boswell, and of the brilliant array of Dutch theologians, lawyers, mathe- maticians and scientists, at whose feet they sat, there is not room to tell here. Perhaps enough has been said however, to indicate something of the debt the two countries owe to each other. Certainly there are remarkable affinities of outlook, temperament and—between Scotland and Friesland —even of language. The Scottish students at Franeker would not be alarmed by the Frisian shibboleth of "bread butter and green cheese" : possibly their broad Doric was intelligible to the innkeepers, landladies and tradesmen of the old Frisian town. We might even hazard a guess that it was they who adapted that shibboleth into the Scottish rhyme :

"Bread, butter and green cheese
Are good Scots and good Fries."

PART OF GLASGOW COLLEGE
Detail from J. Slezer's *Theatrum Scotiae*, 1693

SCIENCE

We have already seen that trade relations had brought Britain into contact with Holland at a number of points. We have seen how trade encouraged navigation, bred up a school of geographers, map-makers and printers; how Englishmen and Scotsmen flocked to the Dutch Universities. From the same interplay of material needs and scientific curiosity, a new school of science was born.

The Royal Society was founded while England was still in the first fine frenzy of royalism, on the crest of a wave of optimistic humanism which made the political and theological controversies of six decades seem arid and unprofitable. Certainly one of the main aims of the Royal Society from its foundation in 1661 was to bring British philosophers, inventors, and experimenters into touch with their contemporaries on the continent. Correspondence with continental philosophers formed the first *Philosophical Transactions* of the Society, and no doubt the appointment of the first Secretary, Henry Oldenburg, a Bremener, was made partly with the object of furthering such correspondence. From the start, then, the Royal Society was universal in its outlook ; more than that, its membership was cosmopolitan. We know from Evelyn, Pepys, and other writers, that there were at this time in England a number of ingenious Dutchmen—men of energy and initiative who brought with them to England that inventiveness and resource for which the Dutch were famous throughout the world. Besides the engineers like Vermuyden, Westerdyke and Croppenburgh, there was Kiviet, who amongst many other projects, had a scheme for popularising a fuel called "loullies," a kind of coal briquette, manufactured at Maastricht. But the most intriguing figure is Cornelius Drebbel, a native of Alkmaar, who came to England in 1604 possibly with Constantijn Huygens. Drebbel was a strange character, half alchemist, half scientist, typical of the early Jacobean age, the age of Donne and the metaphysical poets, an age which could hold both Sir Thomas Browne and Bacon. Drebbel apparently recommended himself to King James, whose love of sorcery was notorious, and was granted an annuity and quarters at Eltham Palace. He rapidly acquired a reputation for "great sagacity as an inventor of machines." Many of his alleged inventions belong to the alchemical side of his genius, but they are worth mentioning as showing the pseudo-scientific interests of contemporary society, and the background of magicians' art from which the scientific revival of the Restoration emerged. He is amongst the many claimants of his time to be the inventor of a machine for producing perpetual motion. He is alleged to have invented a submarine boat which could be navigated from Westminster to Greenwich, and to have made machines to produce rain, hail and lightning. At another time he is said to have invented a device for producing wintry temperatures "of which he made an experiment, as it is pretended, in Westminster Hall at the instance of the King of England: and that the cold was so great as to be unsupportable." No doubt his ingenuity came in useful in staging those fantastically elaborate masques of which James I was so fond. But Drebbel has a claim to be taken more seriously. He turned his attention to devising weapons for naval warfare and was apparently in charge of the fire ships of the expedition to La Rochelle. His masterpiece was however the discovery of a method of dyeing wool scarlet by means of cochineal and tin solutions ; his method was quickly applied at the Gobelin dye works in Paris and later in London at a dye works in Bow. At Leyden his process was used by his son-in-law whose name is variously given as Kuffler, Cuffler, or Keffler, and an interesting link with the Royal Society is formed by their publication in 1662 of an account entitled "an apparatus to the history of the common Practices of Dyeing," which incorporates the work of Drebbel, his son Jacob, and his son-in-law. Needless to say, Drebbel also appears amongst the early projectors connected with the fen drainage schemes. These were only offshoots of what was going on in Holland where, in spite of the dogmatic opposition of the ultra-predestinarian Calvinists, a vigorous school of science had grown up since the beginning of the seventeenth century. It is not surprising therefore, to find that amongst the early members and fellows of the Royal Society there are some distinguished Dutch names. Three of the greatest Dutch scientists—Christiaan Huygens, Antony van Leeuwenhoek, and Herman Boerhaave, accepted Fellowships of the Society. They were all men of broad sympathies and broad vision, and the activities of each covered what nowadays would be regarded as a

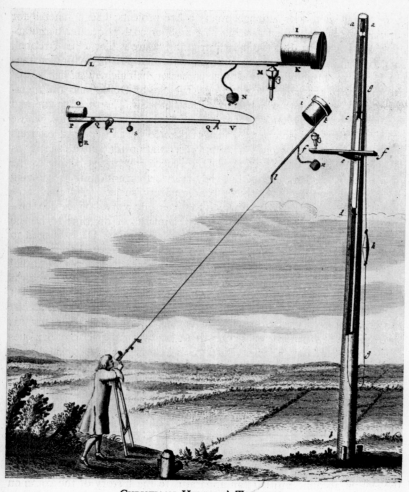

CHRISTIAAN HUYGENS' TELESCOPE
Engraving from Huygens' *Opera Varia*, 1724

number of different fields of scientific investigation. Huygens, for example we now remember primarily as a physicist, but he was also a mathematician, an astronomer and a mechanical scientist. Leeuwenhoek is famous chiefly as a microscopist, but he was also an anatomist and an entomologist. Boerhaave's name was famous throughout the world of medicine, but he was almost as distinguished as a chemist, as a botanist, and as a mathematician. If they were not narrow or specialist in their scientific work, neither were they parochial in their general outlook. As befitted men whose names were known all over Europe, they were good Europeans.

95

Most of Huygens' important discoveries were communicated to the world through the agency of the *Philosophical Transactions* of the Royal Society. Leeuwenhoek made known many of his most striking discoveries to the Royal Society by means of well over a hundred papers communicated to them as well as more than twenty papers communicated to the Paris Academy of Sciences. Huygens and Leeuwenhoek both symbolize the typical contemporary relationship between applied and pure science. Like a number of the early Dutch scientists they both graduated from the school of practical craftsmanship in optical glass technique which had grown up in seventeenth century Holland. This remarkable industry merits a brief description for it is nothing less than the nursery of early Dutch science.

The art of grinding and polishing lenses for telescopes was, of course, of special importance to a community like the Dutch, whose wealth depended on seaborne trade and whose very existence hung on the grain ships which brought the Netherlanders' food from Northern Europe. An elementary knowledge of astronomy was vital to the Dutch seamen and navigators, and whatever their scientists could provide in the way of telescopes, binoculars, spectacles and navigational instruments was welcome to merchants and Government alike. From that need came the scientists, evolving gradually from craftsmen, grinding and polishing lenses for spectacles and telescopes, into applied scientists working to solve practical problems of navigation, and from applied science they moved steadily into the wider spheres of pure science. Perhaps the most important point in this process was the discovery of the telescope in Holland in the early seventeenth century. The discovery itself was for long in dispute. The three claimants were Lippershey and Janssen, the spectacle makers of Middelburg, and Metius, the mathematician of Alkmaar. Examination of the manuscripts in the Huygens' collection at Leyden University has put it beyond dispute that the real inventor was Lippershey, who was given 900 florins by a Committee of the States General, together with a commission to execute two more telescopes of similar design. (Here, as always, the Dutch authorities showed a remarkably modern appreciation of the value of scientific application to the problems of commerce and navigation.) These early Dutch telescopes all consisted of one convex and one concave lens (of the type commonly known as Galilean), and were rapidly found in use in England, as well as in France, Italy and Germany. A few years earlier, Johann and Zacharias Janssen had built the first compound microscope, combining a strong biconcave and a strong biconvex lens. Here then, is one nursery of physical and biological science in seventeenth century Holland. From that nursery came Huygens, who never forgot the art of polishing a lens—an accomplishment which led directly to his great astronomical and physical discoveries ; Leeuwenhoek, who first ground and polished a lens of such short focus as to make possible a simple microscope better than the contemporary compound microscope ;

QUAY OF A DUTCH TOWN
Oil painting by Abraham Storck, 1664

THE STRAND, TOPSHAM, ON THE EXE
Water colour by Hester Frood, 1945

lastly, Boerhaave himself was still close enough to this technical, practical side of science to translate Huygens' treatise on glass polishing into Latin. From these humble and essentially practical beginnings came two of the most notable scientists of the seventeenth century. Christiaan Huygens was born at the Hague in 1629, the son of Constantyn Huygens, Secretary to three Princes of Orange and Lord of Zuylichem. It was, perhaps, from his father that Christiaan Huygens first learned to know of England, for Constantyn, one of the most brilliant and dignified figures in Dutch literature, spent a considerable time in England, studying at Oxford and Cambridge, and was a friend of Donne. Christiaan began his remarkable career at the age of thirteen, when he was already a considerable mathematician and an expert on practical mechanics. Most of Huygens' early work was practical. In 1658 he published his *Brief Demonstration of the Use of the Chronometer for ascertaining Longitude* and demonstrated a model of the newly invented pendulum clock. In 1659 he was at work on a telescope with which he hoped to explain the surprising appearances of Saturn. It was in the course of these observations that he discovered one of Saturn's satellites (Titan) and the existence of Saturn's Rings. The following year he communicated to the Royal Society a paper on the art of polishing lenses for telescopes. He had already used a telescope of twelve feet focal length, while in his *Systema Saturnium* he describes his invention of the micrometer, an instrument which could be used for measuring small angular distances with a telescope or for finding the dimensions of small objects with a microscope. This Huygens used to determine the diameters of planets. By 1681, he was using lenses of enormous focal length to overcome the poor definition characteristic of this type of telescope ; these were mounted on high poles and connected to the eye-piece by means of rods and cords. Three of these object glasses of 123, 180, and 210 feet focal length, are still in the possession of the Royal Society. In another direction, Huygens was experimenting on the newly-invented air-pump into which he introduced a number of improvements ; here again was the beginning of an invention which was to revolutionise the mining industry and ultimately all industrial organisation. Huygens' most important inventions for which he was solely responsible were the micrometer and the pendulum chronometer. Meanwhile, he had evolved a number of scientific principles which rank him with Newton—the laws governing the collision of elastic bodies, the wave theory of light (known as the "Principle of Huygens") and the theory of polarization of light. "He was," writes a biographer "an amiable, cheerful, worthy man : and in all respects as good as he was great. Huygens loved a quiet and studious life, and perhaps through fear of interruption never married."

The basis of Leeuwenhoek's work, like Huygens's, was the perspective instrument, but while Huygens had moved into astronomy, Leeuwenhoek devoted himself to the study of the structure of small bodies with the aid of the microscope. He was introduced to the Royal Society by another great Dutch scientist, Regnier de Graaf, the physiologist, in 1673, and became a Fellow of the Society in 1680. His discoveries were mostly communicated to the world throughout the *Philosophical Transactions*. His list of achievements is truly remarkable. In 1668, he confirmed Malphighi's demonstration of the blood capillaries and in 1674 gave the first accurate description of the red blood corpuscles, which he found to be circular in man, but oval in frogs and fishes. Three years later, he described and illustrated the spermatozoa of animals and investigated the structure of teeth, the crystalline lens, a human muscle, and living and decaying plant organisms. Perhaps his account of the flea, from its first emergence from the egg, is his masterpiece. Other enquiries were into the blighting of trees by *aphides* and into the generation of eels (which contemporary learned men supposed to be produced from the dew without any ordinary processes of generation.) In a superstitious and inaccurate age, when even the scientific ideas of the expert were often mingled with a good deal of mystical mumbo-jumbo, Leeuwenhoek's work is a model of conscientious and accurate scientific research. Leeuwenhoek is buried in the Oude Kerk at Delft, alongside Tromp and Piet Hein. "As everyone, O Wanderer," his epitaph concludes "has respect for old age and wonderful parts, tread this spot with reverence; here lies Science buried with Leeuwenhoek."

Hermann Boerhaave (1668-1738) was elected a Fellow of the Royal Society in 1729, towards the end of a life devoted to medical research and teaching. Boerhaave's election was *honoris causa*. His greatest work was done : in the Netherlands and throughout Europe he was already "the great Boerhaave." Already the story was told of the letter merely addressed "Boerhaave—Europe," which reached its destination safely. Boerhaave was born at Voorhout, a small village about two miles from Leyden. His father intended him to go into the Church, and his first studies at Leyden University were in divinity. But gradually the compass of his reading and activities grew : in addition to theology, he read philosophy, mathematics, botany, and anatomy and chemistry. For a long time, medicine was a hobby with him until gradually his genius became apparent. In 1709 he became Professor of Medicine and Botany, and ten years later, Professor of Chemistry. In these posts, his impressive abilities as a lecturer were devoted to stressing the essential simplicity of true medicine, exploding the fallacies of the alchemists and metaphysical writers and replacing his science on a sound basis of observation and experiment. His published works constitute a vast library of research in medicine, botany and chemistry. With Huygens he is linked by his translation of his papers on the art of lens-making; with Leeuwenhoek by his application of Leeuwenhoek's methods to physiological research. Perhaps his main service to medicine was to reduce it from bad theory to good practice, to bring it down from the dusty bookshelves to the bedside. As Johnson says, Boerhaave was not a theorist—"in his examinations of the sick he was remarkably circumstantial and particular. He well knew the

DE DOORLUCHTIGE SCHOOL.

SCHOOL FOR GENTLEMEN, AMSTERDAM
Engraving c. 1620

originals of Distempers are often at a distance from their visible Effects, that to conjecture where Certainty may be obtained, is either vanity or Negligence, and that Life is not to be sacrificed, either to an Affectation of quick Discernment or of crowded Practice but may be required if trifled away, at the hand of the Physician." In the presence of such humility lesser men than Boerhaave were not afraid to admit that diagnosis was a slow and painful business.

Boerhaave's reputation was considerably enlarged in this country, after his death in 1738, by the brief but superb biography which Samuel Johnson wrote for the *Gentleman's Magazine* in the following year. This most attractive tribute to a most attractive character, which ranks in quality with the *Lives of the Poets*, deserves to be quoted at some length, if only because it is relatively unknown amongst Johnson's works. Obviously Johnson had the highest and most sincere regard for Boerhaave, for this essay is not mere commissioned hack-work : it is Johnson at his best —*nobilmente*. What was it about Boerhaave that attracted Johnson (not usually given to flattery of foreigners) ? I think there were a number of things. Possibly Johnson's love of scientific experiments or his somewhat hypochondriacal interest in medicine introduced him to Boerhaave. Thereafter he was no doubt attracted by certain similarities between Boerhaave's case and his own, by the fortitude with which Boerhaave bore continuous suffering (from a complaint not unlike that from which Johnson himself suffered) by Boerhaave's steady Christian faith and his belief in the efficacy of religion as a strengthening and steadying influence. Undoubtedly,

Johnson was also gratified that in an age when science was already beginning to be identified with atheism or at any rate scepticism, here was a great scientist who well knew where to draw the line between science and religion. But we cannot do better than quote from the last paragraphs of Johnson's biography :

"Thus died Boerhaave, a Man formed by Nature for great Designs, and guided by Religion in the Exertion of his abilities. He was of a robust and athletic Constitution of Body, so harden'd by early Severities, and wholesome Fatigue, that he was insensible of any Sharpness of Air or Inclemency of Weather. . .

"He knew the importance of his own Writings to Mankind, and lest he might, by a Roughness and Barbarity of Stile, too frequent among men of Great Learning, disappoint his own Intentions, and make his Labours less useful, he did not neglect the politer Arts of Eloquence and Poetry. Thus was his learning at once various and exact, profound and agreeable. . .

"So far was this Man from being made Impious by Philosophy, or vain by knowledge, or by Virtue, that he ascribed all his Abilities to the Bounty, and all his Goodness to the Grace of God. May his Example extend its influences to his Admirers and Followers ! May Those who study his writings imitate his life, and those who endeavour after his Knowledge aspire likewise to his Piety."

Boerhaave had, indeed, admirers and followers in many European countries, for both as physician and physiologist he was an inspiring teacher who knew all his pupils individually and maintained a lively and continuous correspondence with many of them. Scottish students and Nonconformists from the North of England especially, flocked to Leyden to study medicine in the wake of their predecessors who had studied law and theology. The majority of the original founders and teachers of the Edinburgh Medical School were pupils of Boerhaave ; John Fothergill (1712-1780) of a Wensleydale Quaker family who became the leader of the new London School of practical medicine was another. In return, Boerhaave always generously acknowledged his debt to contemporary English scientists, especially to Newton and Sydenham, whom he always called "the British Hippocrates." It is almost impossible to overrate the influence of Boerhaave, standing as he does at the beginning of a century which saw such great strides in social medicine and in consequence the beginning of that growth of population which in Britain is linked with an agricultural and industrial revolution destined to transform society.

If the England of 1750 was a different place from the England of 1600, that was largely because men had learned to investigate scientifically phenomena which had previously been screened by a fog of superstition or prejudice. The seventeenth century saw a steady movement from superstition through alchemy to science : and in that movement, Dutch scientists —some of them working closely with the Royal Society—played an important part.

ON A DUTCH CANAL
Oil painting by Aert van der Neer, 1603-1677

DUTCH INFLUENCE ON THE ENGLISH COUNTRYSIDE

The seventeenth century Englishman seems to have derived intense amusement from the reflection that Holland had been reclaimed from the sea. A land below sea-level ! Marvell in his *Character of Holland* sets to work to do a satirical justice to a country where :

> "The fish oft times the burger dispossest
> And sat, not as a meat, but as a guest."

where,

> "Not who first sees the rising sun, commands,
> But who could first discern the rising lands ;
> Who best could know to pump an earth so leak
> Him they their Lord, and Country's Father, speak :
> To make a bank was a great Plot of State,
> Invent a Shov'l and be a Magistrate."

It was a poor joke, smacking strongly of sour grapes, for England was still apprenticed to the Dutch not only in matters of trade, finance, printing, science, architecture, and painting, but even in engineering itself. Many of our own engineering and reclamation works of this

SKATERS ON A CANAL : WINTER
Oil painting by Aert van der Neer, 1603-1677

period were carried out by Dutch technicians. The first successful project
for supplying London with drinking water in 1582 was carried out by one
Peter Morice, a Dutchman, who erected a pumping engine in the first
arch of London Bridge, worked by water wheels which forced the water
through lead pipes into the houses. The force of water was such that
Morice was able to throw water "over St. Magnus's steeple, greatly to
the astonishment of the Mayor and Aldermen, who assembled to witness
the experiment." A little later we find Johannes Croppenburgh and a
company of Dutch workmen reclaiming and embanking Canvey Island
near the mouth of the Thames, while Cornelius Vandervelt enclosed
Wapping Marsh by means of a high bank along which the present High
Street was made. At Yarmouth, Jansen, another Dutchman, was employed
to construct the new harbour, while the enclosure of Brading Haven in
the Isle of Wight was carried out by Sir Hugh Myddelton in 1620 with the
aid of "Dutchmen brought out of the Low Countries." It was in connection
with the repair of a breach in the Thames Embankment at Dagenham in
1621 that we first hear of the greatest of the Dutch immigrant engineers,
Cornelius Vermuyden. Vermuyden was a native of Zeeland and an experienced embanking engineer. The success of his operations at Dagenham
led to a contract to drain the Royal Park at Windsor. There he became
known to the King who shortly after employed him on the first of the
two great projects which occupied the rest of his life, brought him fame
and notoriety, ruined his health and finally brought him in old age to

A VILLAGE WITH WATER MILLS : SUMMER
Oil painting by Meindert Hobbema, 1638-1709

poverty and disappointment : this was the drainage of Hatfield Chase on the borders of Yorkshire : the second project for the drainage of the Lincoln and Cambridge Fens was even more ambitious. The contract for the drainage of the Chase was drawn up on May 24th, 1626, Vermuyden undertaking to make the drowned lands fit for tillage and pasturage. In return he was to have one third of the reclaimed land. The adventure was financed by a company composed chiefly of Dutchmen—Mathew Valkenburgh, the Van Peenens, John Corsellis and others. The workmen were also mainly Dutch or Flemish, drawn from the Colonies at Dagenham and Canvey Island. But the ill-luck which was to dog Vermuyden's later ventures beset him almost at once. There was continuous and violent opposition to his plans from the local inhabitants, who disliked the alien invasion and mistrusted—possibly rightly—the objects of the adventurers. In spite of this local opposition, which smouldered for fifteen years, much was achieved including the cutting of the dyke called the Dutch River, which took the waters of the Don directly into the Ouse, near Goole. Vermuyden was well supported by Charles I, who honoured him with a knighthood in 1629, and for some years, the new settlers cultivated their lands in peace, building their own cottages and churches and peopling the lonely flats with windmills in the Dutch manner. But the shadow of civil dissension was gradually darkening the land, and Vermuyden as a royal protegee and a foreigner, with all his schemes, was suspect. The opposition flared up one night in 1642, when the Parliamentarians at Lincoln received news that the Royalists were about to march into the Isle of Axholme from Yorkshire. Orders were given to break the dykes and pull up the sluice gates ; the floods roared out and over the land and in a few hours the work of years was undone.

In the meantime, Vermuyden had been in contact with the Earl of Bedford, trying to set on foot his plan for reclaiming the Cambridge Fens. In this he found himself in competition with another Dutchman, Wester-dyke, who also submitted plans, but Vermuyden's superior organising ability and wider experience apparently won the day. A formidable task faced him : the watery wastes from Boston to Ely were inhabited by the "fen-slodgers"—a wild, strange people even more hostile to change than the inhabitants of Hatfield Chase. Vermuyden's workmen were attacked and their works pulled down : the streets and inns of Holbeach, Wisbech, Chatteris and Ely rang to the ominous sounds of ballads like the following :

"The Dutchman hath a thirsty soul,
Our cellars are subject to his call ;
Let every man, then, lay hold on his bowl,
'Tis pity the German sea should have all.
Then apace, apace drink, drink deep, drink deep,
Whilst to be had let's the liquor ply ;
The draines are up, and a coile they'll keep,
And threaten to drain the Kingdom dry.
Why should we stay here and perish with thirst ?
To the new world in the moon away let us goe,
For if the Dutch Colony get thither first,
'Tis a thousand to one but they'll drain that too."

Vermuyden's schemes suffered disaster : under cover of the prevailing civil disorders, his banks and dykes were broken down and by 1642 the greater part of the Fens again lay waste. It was not until 1649, after another triumph over his opponents (including once more his Dutch rival Wester-dyke) that the work began again. By 1652 the works were declared to be complete and at Ely, Vermuyden read to the Lords Commissioners an address in which he claimed that in the North and Middle Levels, there were already 40,000 acres of reclaimed land "sown with cole-seed, wheat and other winter grain besides innumerable quantities of sheep, cattle and other stock." He concluded, "I humbly desire that God may have the glory, for His blessing and bringing to perfection my poor endeavours, at the vast charge of the Earl of Bedford and his participants." Soon after-wards, Vermuyden disappears from sight, a broken and disappointed man ; but in spite of his failures, his achievements were considerable. A boggy wilderness was replaced by hundreds of thousands of acres of the best land in Britain and broad fields of corn waved where formerly only the wild fowl screamed and dived over the reeds and waters. Vermuyden has been the victim not merely of his contemporaries and his own poverty but

WINDMILLS
Chalk drawing by John Sell Cotman, 1806

of succeeding generations of academic critics. It has been continually alleged that he did not appreciate the difference between the problems of his native Zeeland (where the difficulty was to keep out the ocean) and that of the Fens, where it was to provide a ready outfall in face of the continual silting up of the wash. The verdict of present day engineers is different : it is now held that Vermuyden's plan of 1652 was substantially right : certainly there is a striking similarity between it and Sir Murdoch Macdonald's flood protection scheme of 1940 which was fully backed up by Mr. Doran, the Chief Engineer of the Great Ouse Catchment Board. (It is interesting too that the Board has of late years employed a British Company of Dutch parentage working to the plans and methods of a Rotterdam engineer.) Vermuyden has, in fact, been largely vindicated. Not until the nineteenth century did Britain repay something of her debt to Dutch skill, when John Rennie, who may be said to have completed Vermuyden's work, applied Watts's steam-engine to water pumping in place of the windmill. The same process was later extended to the Netherlands, and resulted in the draining of 45,000 acres of the Haarlemer Meer. The disappearance of Vermuyden does not quite spell the end of Dutch effort in the Fens. In John Evelyn's Diary, we read of a Dutch acquaintance

DENVER SLUICES, LINCOLNSHIRE
Pencil and wash drawing by Henry Rushbury, 1925

PROJECT FOR A NEW SLUICE AT IJMUIDEN
Wash drawing by J. Enonar

of Evelyn's, Kiviet, whose plan for wharfing the Thames Evelyn put to the King in an effort to gain his patronage. In another place the inventive Kiviet is described as undertaking, together with Lord Wotton, "to drain the meres and grow hemp and cole seed" at Newmarket.

But the Dutch did not only show us the way to reclaim our drowned acres from the sea ; they also showed us how to plant, cultivate and graze them. Unfortunately, it is almost impossible to be exact or categorical about innovations in agrarian history ; we are drawn inevitably into a world of rural legend, of stories which betook a slightly fuddled way from one inn to the next, and anecdotes handed down from father to son, until it is difficult to discern with any certainty where new fashions and methods began or who began them.

Nevertheless, even legend has its own importance and the number of times the Dutchman appears in the shadowy annals of our farming history in these years is significant. As one would expect, the references are usually connected with the development of root crops or the scientific breeding of cattle. Antony Ashley, grandfather of the Earl of Shaftesbury, spent some time in the Netherlands and transcribed some of the works of the great cartographer, Lucas Wagenaer (the author of the *Spieghel der Zeevaert*. Another achievement with which he is credited was the introduction of the cabbage into England from the Netherlands. But rural England of Stuart times was in no mood to abandon its normal and characteristic chaos for the methodical and scientific ways of the Dutch ; too many country squires were away at the wars and too many estates devastated by sword and fire or ruined by debt. Another hundred years passed, therefore, before those changes were wrought which were to transform English farming—changes which, in the last resort, may fairly be ascribed to Dutch influence. The chief one was the process whereby clover and turnips were embodied into the crop-rotation. This not only made for an efficient and economical method of combined arable and stock farming but also prepared the way for the later achievements of Bakewell and Curwen in developing new and improved strains of cattle and sheep. It is certain that both crops had been in systematic use in the Netherlands for many years, and it seems more than likely that Lord Townshend ("Turnip" Townshend as he became known) who had been Ambassador to the United Provinces and who is usually given the credit for their introduction on a large scale, had noted in his painstaking way how successfully the Dutch used them. Great quantities of clover-seed were imported in these years from Amsterdam by West Country merchants. The seed was usually unloaded from the Dutch ships on to the quays at Topsham about April to be sold at Exeter or Tiverton Markets in time for the sowing season. There it was bought by the travelling chapmen who distributed to their customers all over Devon, Somerset, Dorset and Wiltshire.

According to Vermuyden's opponents, the crops which he and his fellow engineers planned to grow on their reclaimed land—cole-seed and rape seed—also came from the Netherlands ; to them they were "but Dutch commodities and but trash and trumpery."

At the same time the famous breed of Frisian cattle was making its appearance in Britain. Mortimer, writing in 1707, remarked that "the long-legged short-horned Cow of the Dutch breed" found in Lincolnshire and Kent was the best breed for milking. By the end of the century great strides had been made and the famous Lincolnshire red short-horn emerged as the final triumphant combination of the Dutch and Northern English strains.

Nor must we overlook the more exotic exports from Holland. Many an English merchant from London or the West country, visiting his Amsterdam correspondent to look over samples of linens from Germany or silks from Italy would bring back a selection of bulbs for his garden, chosen for him perhaps by his Dutch friends from the *bollenvelden* at Haarlem or Bloemendaal. And tradition has it that it was Sir Matthew Decker, a wealthy Dutch financier who settled at Richmond, became a Member of Parliament and acquired a great reputation for philanthropy, who grew the first pineapple on English soil.

As we come to the great corn-growing era of English farming in the later eighteenth and the nineteenth centuries, Dutch influence wanes, for the Netherlands had always been great importers of corn, reserving their own soil for more specialised and profitable crops. But in the second decade of this century, and again after the war of 1914-18, when years of ruinous competition from across the Atlantic had at last forced the British farmer to specialise and experiment once again, the pioneers of sugar beet cultivation called in expert assistance and capital from Holland ; and it is not altogether coincidence that it was to Vermuyden's lands—the lands of bulbs and roots—that a good many of these, the latest of the Dutch invaders of Britain, came after very nearly three hundred years.

VICE-ADMIRAL WYBRANT VAN WARWICK ON THE ISLAND OF BANDA
Engraving of the Dutch East Indies, 1598

EXPLORATION AND COLONIAL TRADE

It was not only in Europe that the seventeenth century Englishman came up against the thorough-going energy and persistence of the Dutch in their pursuit of trade. From the banks of the Hudson River to Bantam and the Moluccas, the English trader found himself in competition with his Dutch rival, haggling with the American Indian for beaver pelts or alternately flattering and bullying some Eastern prince in pursuit of a spice monopoly. In exploration, the English might well have claimed priority in certain fields : but it was the Dutch who, at any rate in the Malay Archipelago, consolidated their trading position with a singleness of purpose which their English rivals lacked. Here, more than in the West, trade rivalries showed themselves in all their naked unloveliness. Amongst tropical climates and the continual hazards and insecurity of the Europeans' existence tempers became quick, while contact with oriental savagery did nothing to mitigate the brutality which was never very deeply hidden beneath the veneer of seventeenth century civilization.

The first Dutch expedition to the East Indies, henceforth to be the chief field of Dutch colonial trade, left the Texel on April 2nd, 1595. Four ships sailed out under the command of Cornelius Houtman, accompanied by the roar of artillery and the enthusiastic cheers of the crowds assembled on shore. The voyage was financed by a group of Amsterdam merchants who had taken good care to acquire all the information they could about the earlier journeys of Drake and Cavendish, and where possible to secure the services of seamen or pilots who had served on those expeditions. Amongst those on board were John Davis and James Lancaster, there presumably to learn the navigation. Six years later, these two were to be in charge of the English East India Company's first expedition to the same waters. After a long and weary voyage, beset by gales and hurricanes, and decimated by scurvy, the expedition reached the Sunda Straits in February 1596 and Bantam on June 23rd. Other expeditions followed and in 1602, the various interests of Holland and Zealand combined to form the Dutch East India Company, with the blessing of the States General.

In 1603, the English opened a factory, or "house of trade" at Bantam. A few months later, the Dutch followed their example. Both sides already had establishments at Amboyna in the Moluccas. At Batavia too, the Dutch and English factories faced one another. Friction increased and nothing which diplomacy could do in London and the Hague was able to curb the development of an ugly situation, which culminated in the infamous incident at Amboyna. The fact was that both sides were obsessed with the importance of colonial trade as a source of wealth and sea power and were prepared to go to any lengths in their efforts to secure a monopoly of the trade in sugar, pepper, spices, rice, indigo and rare fabrics, the rich prize offered by the Eastern seas.

But nowhere in the Archipelago did English affairs flourish as did those of their rivals. At Bantam the English community was dogged by disease and ill-fortune ; at Amboyna the massacre of 1622 put an end to English prestige ; at Batavia, the energy of the Dutch Governor, Jan Pieterzoon Coen, quickly reduced the English merchants' position to one of mere sufferance. In the Moluccas, the Dutch continued to have their own troubles with native chiefs but in the end they had their own way, and the English and Portuguese were excluded by treaty from trading with the native princes at any port whatsoever. The spice monopoly was secured, and with this monopoly the Dutch controlled the supply and the price level of spices for the entire European market. Finally in 1682, the English factory at Bantam was closed and the history of the English Company in Java comes to an end. We are at the beginning of a process of separation into English and Dutch "spheres of influence" in the East, a process which in the end meant that the Dutch occupied the Archipelago, while the English took to the mainland of Asia, establishing themselves in factories and ports in every useful area from the Red Sea to China, not only at Surat, Bombay, Madras and Calcutta but at dozens of smaller stations too. While Dutch fortunes were in the ascendant in the Archipelago, they were on the wane elsewhere. The profitable trade of Formosa, which they captured from the Portuguese in 1624 and held until 1664, was lost to a Chinese pirate in that year. Elsewhere, the Dutch held out until the Napoleonic period, though with declining fortunes. Ceylon was lost to the

English in 1796 ; the monopoly of the Javanese trade ended with the English conquest of Java in 1811 ; Malacca, on the West coast of the Malay peninsula was taken by the English in 1795 but returned in 1819. In 1824, however, the Dutch exchanged it with England for the Residency of Bencoolen in Sumatra. Finally, in 1819, the great colonial administrator, Sir Stamford Raffles, had lighted upon the ancient city of Singapore as a potential centre for Britain's Indian trade. The project was pushed on vigorously in face of the opposition of a powerful combination of interests, the Penang Government and the Dutch being strongly against him, and the Government at home lukewarm to say the least of it : but Raffles's foresight had finally determined the shape which the European settlement of the East was to take for more than a hundred years. Hardly less important than his selection of Singapore were his administrative achievements during the British occupation of Java. Raffles succeeding in winning the loyalty of his Dutch colleagues : after his death reaction set in and Raffles's name became mud. Later, Liberal Dutch colonial administrators like Thorbecke and Van Deventer turned again to place him on a pedestal. Nowadays, it is generally recognised that although some of Raffles's policies were opportunist, he was the first to aim at a genuine improvement in native welfare, the first who sincerely tried to temper profit-hunting with philanthropy. He was, in fact, the pioneer of modern colonial administration in Netherlands India.

The British retreat to the Indian mainland is one of the fundamental events in British imperial history for it shaped the whole future of British trade and influence in Asia. Why did it come about? Two explanations have been put forward. The old view was that the Dutch beat the English out of the Archipelago by superior ability, greater energy and a profusion of expenditure on forts and warships which made their position there impregnable and uncontestable. The English thereupon retreated to the mainland as a second and unavoidable choice. More recently another explanation has been given. Supporters of this theory take the view that whereas the Dutch concentrated on the spice trade of the Archipelago—the pepper of Sumatra and Java, and the cloves and nutmegs of the Moluccas—the English traders were in search of markets for English textiles and manufactures and were accordingly more interested in the thickly populated mainland of Asia. If that is so, it may explain the comparative lack of drive shown by the English in the Archipelago, for there is little doubt that they were outwitted at every point by the Dutch in the spice islands. Ultimately the importance of spices decreased while the English traders were working up a great import trade of Persian silks, Indian cottons, calicoes, chintzes and muslins, dyes, Bengal saltpetre, coffee from Mocha and the valuable tea trade from China. It is only in the last fifty years or so that under an enlightened Dutch colonial administration a wide range of mineral and agricultural production has replaced the old spice and indigo culture. By the end of the eighteenth century, both the great East India Companies, Dutch and British, had fallen into decline. The Dutch Company paid its last dividend in 1782, and in 1798, its affairs were taken over by the Government. Like its rival Company, it had become little more than a façade cloaking the individual enterprises of private individuals within the Company's brotherhood.

In the meantime, other Dutch discoveries had taken place which were to have consequences of even greater moment to the British Empire. These were the opening up of the South West Pacific and the settlements on the Atlantic coast of America. There was a tradition that south of New Guinea lay a great continent—a tradition which possibly originated in half-remembered tales of earlier voyagers, possibly in the old theory that the southern hemisphere must contain as much land as the northern in order to maintain the stability of the earth—a nice instance of how the Middle Ages occasionally came to the right conclusion for the wrong reason. In 1606 came the first authenticated discovery of Australia by the Dutchman Willem Janszoon who, coming from Bantam in the *Duifken*, crossed the dangerous region of shoals and islands separating New Guinea from Australia and penetrated into the Gulf of Carpentaria, reaching the west coast of Queensland. The Dutch explorers were not impressed by what they found in these lands of promise ; they wrote :

"This extensive country, for the greatest part desert, but in some places inhabited by wild, cruel, black savages, by whom some of the crew were murdered ; for which reason they could not learn anything of the land or waters, as had been desired of them, and, by want of provisions and other necessaries, they were obliged to leave the discovery unfinished; the furthest point of the land was called in their Map, Cape Keer-Weer (Cape Turn-Again)."

Ten years later, the Dutch accidentally discovered Western Australia. A Dutch ship taking the route south of the tropics from the Cape of Good Hope to Java overran the passage westwards before turning north to Java and sighted the west coast of Australia. During the following decade, the whole of the west coast was charted, and in 1627 another Dutch ship explored about half the southern coast. The new continent was christened *New Holland*, but thereafter Dutch interest flagged; Janszoon's successors conceived no more affection for it than he. It promised no spices, food or even fresh water. Meanwhile other Dutch seamen were exploring in the north and in 1623, one had crossed the Gulf of Carpentaria and discovered Arnhem Land.

Dutch enterprise in the South West Pacific culminated in the voyages of the great commander and navigator Abel Tasman and his chief pilot and planner, Frans Visscher, sailing under the patronage of the Governor General of the East Indies, Antony van Diemen. The immediate motive of the expedition was strategic ; in South America the Dutch were at grips with the Spaniards ; their problem was to find access to the Spanish colonies in South America without having to go all the way round the

THE APPROACH OF WINTER IN WARTIME HOLLAND
Water colour by Albert Richards, 1944

TULIP FIELDS SEEN THROUGH THE GATEWAY OF A DUTCH TOWN
L.N.E.R. Poster by Yunge, 1933

North Pacific and down the Californian coast, risking the twin hazards of calms and adverse winds. Tasman's aim was to steer a passage south of Australia ; his voyage brought him to an island (Tasmania) which he named van Diemen land ; then, turning east into the open ocean, he came to an unknown land which he called New Zealand. He followed the coastline to its most northerly point which he called after his patron's wife, Maria van Diemen, then, convinced that the west wind track to South America was navigable, he sailed back to Batavia by the northern coast of New Guinea.

Tasman's discoveries entitle him to be called the greatest explorer since Magellan ; they were not to be surpassed in importance until the time of Cook. As a result of his voyages and those of his predecessors, the Dutch had come to know a great deal about Western and Northern Australia, though they still mistakenly believed New Guinea to be contiguous with North East Australia. They also knew the southern coast as far east as Tasmania. But these were not the most attractive or fertile stretches of the new continent ; the eastern half of the south coast and the east coast— the regions which make up the greater part of the populated Dominion to-day—remained outside the scope of their knowledge and interest. Obsessed by the narrow conception of colonial trade as a quest for spices, the Dutch explorers were blind to the vast potentialities of these continents which they discovered, charted and left sprinkled with Dutch names which have survived to this day.

For sixty years after Tasman's great voyage, interest in New Holland and New Zealand languished, to be revived at the end of the century by a reformed English buccaneer, William Dampier. Another half century was to pass, however, before England produced the greatest of all the South Sea explorers, Captain James Cook, a sailor by profession, a brilliant cartographer and a man of powerful intellect and sterling character, under whose influence the South West Pacific finally became a sphere of British development.

Trade to the East had brought into prominence another area long to be associated with Dutch settlement. The Cape of Good Hope was discovered by Bartholomew Diaz in 1488 but it was not until 1652 that the Dutch set up a fortress and victualling station there under a naval surgeon, Jan van Riebeeck. The situation was of great strategic importance to the Dutch East India Company, which accordingly governed the settlement with an iron despotism. Far from encouraging immigration and development, the Company restricted rights and privileges narrowly to its own servants ; so far from allowing any growth of self-government or political liberty, all power was concentrated in the hands of the Company's Governor, whose word was law. The Cape Colony was, in fact, one of the least happy examples of Dutch colonial settlement ; in every particular, the actions of the Company ran counter to traditions and ideals commonly regarded as the heritage of Holland.

"Trekking," the phenomenon of South African life which we usually associate with the nineteenth century, actually began in the late seventeenth century, when the more independently minded settlers, refusing to tolerate the oppression of the Company, set off north to breathe a freer and more congenial atmosphere. But the tyrannical government of the Company left an evil heritage. Old antipathies were multiplied by British occupation in 1795. In 1814, temporary occupation was transformed into permanent cession—cession that rested on the sanctions of conquest, of treaty and of purchase—on every sanction, that is to say, except consideration for the preferences of the inhabitants. A century of secession and conflict followed, and South Africa seemed doomed to misery and disunity. The first promise of better things was not fulfilled. In the febrile anxiety of a dying man to complete his life's work, Rhodes shattered his own high hopes and alienated and disillusioned his supporters among the Cape Dutch—one of them was Jan Christian Smuts. The dream of a united South Africa turned into the nightmare of the Boer War. The revelation of South African wealth whetted capitalist appetites ; British electors and governors were ignorant of African conditions and problems. The philanthropic horror of the Liberals at the Boer native policy combined easily with the provocative arrogance of the Uitlanders. All this merely stiffened the Boers in their usual obstinacy. Yet both sides showed deeper and more noble qualities, almost in spite of themselves. Within a short time of the war's ending, the Campbell Bannerman Government took the unbelievably bold decision to grant self-government. From the Dutch side came statesmen like Botha, Reitz and Smuts, men determined to weld a new nation from the bitterness and conflict. The work is slow and the problems and set-backs many. But their patience and wisdom has not been in vain. Not long before his death, the late Col. Denys Reitz prophesied that "within the next thirty years or so even our most fervid racial politicians will find it hard to distinguish an Englishman from a Dutchman. We will all have become South Africans without distinction of race or origin."

In the settlement of the Atlantic Coast of America too the Dutch played an important part. In 1609, two years after Christopher Newport had brought his battered ships into Chesapeake Bay and initiated the English settlement of America, Henry Hudson sailed west in search of a North West Passage to India. It was a curious example of Anglo-Dutch partnership, for Hudson, an Englishman, was in the employment of the Amsterdam Chamber of the Dutch East India Company. Hudson failed to find what he was looking for ; instead he found the river which bears his name, which he believed to be the opening of a channel which would bring him out into the Pacific. When his supposition proved wrong, his backers lost interest, but already the possibilities of the fur trade had attracted the notice of other merchants. A New Netherlands Company was founded ; blockhouses flying the Dutch flag sprang up, one on the island of

Manhattan, another—"Orange"—where Albany now is. With that unerring instinct for selecting an *entrepôt* site which led them to Batavia and St. Eustatius, the Dutch gained in New Amsterdam an unrivalled position for controlling trade on the Atlantic seaboard. They had a firm grip on another trade essential to the development of the Southern States and the West Indies. By 1640 the Dutch from the Gold Coast were pumping a stream of negro labour into the West Indian sugar plantations. Altogether, New Amsterdam was too great a temptation to the English settlers : while a continual stream of English emigrants was rapidly expanding the New England and Virginian settlements, the Dutch settlement in between remained small and backward. Holland could not provide a supply of colonists comparable to the flow of emigrants, first Puritan then Cavalier, who were swarming to America between 1629 and 1660. Perhaps the very virtues of Holland—tolerance and liberty—were an obstacle to colonial expansion. Holland was too prosperous and pleasant a land to leave in favour of the terrors and hardships of an unknown continent. It is a remarkable fact that the greatest Dutch "coloniser" of the period, Kiliaen van Rensselaer, died without setting foot in America ; all his plans were directed from Amsterdam. As a result of the war of 1664-7, New Amsterdam became New York, and its seven thousand Dutch inhabitants became —fairly willingly for the most part—subjects of the Crown. The strategic position of New York made it invaluable for enforcing the Navigation Acts, and it was not returned to its owners. Simultaneously, Britain's grip on the African coast was strengthened and in 1672 the Royal African

Company ousted the Dutch from their position as the recognised slave traffickers to the plantations.

Although New Amsterdam was lost, the Dutch left impressions on the settlement which were not easily erased. The traditional love of holidays and feast days was reflected in New York's noisy New Year's Day, when much was eaten, more was drunk, and great was the demand for transport in the early hours. Personal ties with Holland remained strong ; as late as 1795, a giant speculation in land in Pennsylvania and New York was floated by a Dutch group called *De Hollandsche Land Compagnie*. And when John Adams went in search of a loan for the Confederate Government, it was to Amsterdam that he turned, reminding the States-General a trifle irritably that :

"The originals of the two Republicks are so much alike that the history of the one seems but a transcript from that of the other, so that every Dutchman instructed in the subject must pronounce the American Revolution just and necessary, or pass censure upon the greatest actions of his immortal ancestors."

It was an American of Dutch descent who cut the Erie Canal ("Clinton's Ditch") and poured the first kegful of Lake water into the Atlantic ; it was the first of the famous members of the Roosevelt family, Nicholas, who ran the first steamboat service from Pittsburgh to New Orleans. The Dutch did not quickly forget their traditional skills.

To summarise ; within half a century of their earliest voyages, Dutch traders and adventurers had sketched the future course of European colonial development. They had laid the foundations of an Eastern and a Western Empire : they had established a settlement in the pleasant lands of South Africa and another on the Atlantic seaboard of America : they had discovered and charted considerable stretches of territory in Australia and New Zealand. Yet the Hollanders' enterprise failed to live up to its early promise. Except for the East Indies and some islands and territories in the West Indies and South America, the Dutch settlements either stagnated, or fell supinely before the aggressive enterprise of new comers, or simply failed to take root. A variety of causes contributed to these failures. In the first place, the Dutch colonies were purely trading posts ; not even the wealth poured out on the fortifications and warships for the defence of the East Indies altered this fact. Moreover the conception of trade behind the settlements was often limited by preconceived ideas— the collection of some staple article of trade—spices for preference—with a view to resale in Europe. Lands which did not yield spices were not likely to arouse much interest. The *entrepôt* system took hold overseas as at home. The middleman conception flourished ; the pioneer spirit was rare. The loneliness of the log-cabin and the dangers of the pathfinder's trail did not appeal to town dwellers from the most wealthy, the most thickly populated and most highly urbanised corner of Europe, who were for the most part content to leave these fields of lonely glory to their fellow Calvinists from Scotland. In his own land the Dutchman had shown no lack of enterprise or vigour, rescuing a land from the ocean and creating wealth out of nothing. But this small and tranquil corner of Europe, perhaps because of its size or its tranquillity, perhaps because its energies had been concentrated on the long struggle at home, failed to supply the flow of hardy emigrants necessary fully to sustain an era of colonial expansion. Finally, the great trading Companies kept a stranglehold on the overseas settlements which choked enterprise and discouraged emigration. So the Cape Colony was stillborn and New Amsterdam was swept into the British Empire on a surging tide of colonial expansion, the same tide which a hundred years later was to carry the whole Atlantic settlement clean out of that Empire once again. In Australia and New Zealand, on the Atlantic seaboard of America, in Ceylon and the Carribbean, the British were to reap the full harvest of colonial wealth and Imperial power from the early sowings of the Dutch navigators and settlers, though the marks of the Dutchman remain to the present day. Finally in South Africa there is promise of a new national unity to which Dutch and English can make free and equal contribution. In the East, Dutch squadrons are flying American planes from Australian bases : an augury, it may be hoped, of co-operation which will endure and thrive with peace.

CURACAO, DUTCH WEST INDIES
Oil painting by A. van Anrooy

DUTCH COAT OF ARMS
From Wagenaer's Atlas, 1588

CONCLUSION

Between the Treaty of Utrecht and the Treaty of Vienna many things happened to change drastically the pattern of Dutch economy and Holland's relations with the rest of the world. Britain herself achieved economic maturity and threw off that dependence on Dutch shipping and Dutch skill which had done much to shape our history in the previous century. More than that, British industry had undergone great changes in technique and organisation which, linked with the operations of a mighty Navy and an expanding Imperialism, enabled her to defeat the Napoleonic design to dominate Europe. In this new world of iron and steel where immense navies and vast national armies clashed in battle, the Dutch, ill-supplied with natural resources and with a relatively small population, were inevitably outnumbered and outfought. In the face of the economic aggressiveness of Britain's Navigation Acts and the general inclination towards nationalist economies, the old multilateral trading system which had made the Dutch the carriers, brokers and middlemen of Europe tottered and collapsed. The military disasters of the last decades of the eighteenth century and the early years of the nineteenth century completed the dissolution of the old order.

In the war of 1780 to 1783, the Francophile elements in Holland succeeded in bringing the Dutch into the war against Britain. The crowning disaster came at Camperdown in October 1797 when the Dutch Fleet at the Texel was ordered to sea to disable Admiral Duncan's Squadron, hardly yet recovered from the effects of the recent mutinies. The sides were evenly matched—sixteen battleships against sixteen. In the battle that followed, one of the most bitter and bloody in naval history, the Dutch fought, as they had always done, with superb skill and courage, but after three hours the Dutch Admiral de Winter was compelled to strike his flag. Half his battleships were captured ; the remainder escaped, to be taken two years later by Admiral Mitchell. The proud Dutch Fleet had been shattered in the last of a series of great actions in which the Royal Navy had encountered sailors of their own calibre, men compared with whom Medina Sidonia, Villeneuve and their crews were but amateurs. When the Dutch Navy appears again in English history it is by the side of the Royal Navy with Admiral Doorman in the dogged, tragic Battle of the Java Sea, with the gallant Dutch submarines and destroyers in the Mediterranean struggle, with the dashing Dutch gunboats that bombarded the coasts of Italy and Normandy in the Allied operations of 1943 and 1944.

During the land campaigns that followed Camperdown, Holland became a battle-ground for British, Russian and French armies in the abortive Den Helder campaign. The great trade of Holland was reduced to practically nothing : the great warehouses of Amsterdam were empty and grass grew in the cobbled streets ; there was starvation in the granary of Europe and overseas the great Dutch Empire was crumbling away.

The last three years of the struggle (1810-1813) saw great changes. Previously Holland had been left more or less to her own devices ; now, with annexation to the French Empire, came French control and compulsory service in the French Army and Navy. Resistance, at first unorganised and sporadic, became stronger as the situation of the French grew more desperate. G. K. van Hogendorp, a patrician of high standing with many English connections, became the centre of organised resistance.

FIREWORKS ON THE THAMES CELEBRATING THE PEACE OF UTRECHT, 1713
Contemporary engraving

An underground system of propaganda was organised, based on London, where the Prince of Orange and his family were living in exile. Newspapers and broadsheets filtered through by a number of channels. The Amsterdam banking house of Baring and Hope, which kept in constant touch with its London Office, was one post in an efficient intelligence service. Fast yachts from England would appear off the Dutch fishing grounds with bales of broadsheets, newspapers and posters which were delivered by the fishermen to destinations in Holland as far east as Utrecht. All this propaganda paved the way for liberation and the restoration of the House of Orange. When the higher French officials finally fled and van Hogendorp formed a provisional government, it was to England that he turned for help.

By this time, a profound change had overtaken relations between the two countries. The flow of capital, which for two centuries had been outwards from Holland had been reversed. British money, British capital goods and British skill began to flow to Holland as to a dozen other countries. Two years after his restoration, the King of the Netherlands went into partnership with John Cockerill, the man who more than any other single individual was the creator of modern industrial Belgium. (Cockerill was given the chateau of the Prince Bishop of Liége at Seraing for his machine works.) The Belgian Revolution of 1830 screened Holland from the full impact of British migrant capital but left her susceptible to some of its attractions. At the peak of the financial crisis of 1837, a loan to Holland was floated in London. By 1850, British gas companies were operating in Holland, supplying Amsterdam and Rotterdam, and in 1851, British capital built a water system for the city of Amsterdam. Much more recently, great sums of British money have been invested in Netherlands India. These are a few symbols of the changing economic order. The great lender had turned borrower—and ideas as well as capital were among the borrowings.

The overflow of British wealth was in itself a sign of the stability and prosperity which Britain had achieved under a new form of government, a government in which constitutional monarchy was linked with a reformed Parliament and a liberal democracy. And while the ideas of the French Revolution were a powerful force in Dutch politics, it is undeniable that the working model of British liberalism provided another powerful stimulus to progress. William I, partly educated at Oxford, was especially susceptible to English ideas. Under William II, the fundamental law was altered in the direction of constitutional monarchy. William III occupied a place in the constitutional development of Holland and in the affections of his people not unlike that of Edward VII in our own. And what Queen Victoria at her Jubilee meant to England, that Queen Wilhemina means to the Dutch people to-day. (The film *Victoria Regina* played to packed houses for many weeks in Holland in 1937. Its reception by Dutch audiences—not usually given to outward show of emotion—was quite

DUTCH LACEMAKERS
Pencil drawing by A. van Anrooy

extraordinary.) To this fortunate succession of able governors must also
be added the traditional political good sense of the Dutch. In an earlier
century, Sir William Temple had a word to say about this :

"In these assemblies," (he writes) "though all are equal in Voices, and
any one hinders a result ; yet it seldom happens, but that united by a
common bond of interest, and having all one common End of Publique
Good, They come after full Debates to Easie Resolutions; yielding to
the power of Reason where it is clear and strong; And suppressing all
private Passions or interests so as the smaller part seldom contests hard
and long what the greater agrees of."

National characteristics change but slowly. In nineteenth century
Holland, as in nineteenth century England, this good sense made it possible to fuse monarchist aspirations and patrician leadership with the
demand for popular representation and to create successful constitutional
forms of government. More recently, in the dangerous pre-war years, it
enabled the free institutions of Holland to withstand successfully the
attempts of a small but energetic Fascist minority to set up a pro-German
dictatorship. No amount of tub-thumping or heel-clicking could prevail

BRITISH TRANSPORT CROSSING THE FLOODED MAAS
Water colour by Albert Richards, 1944

against the biting mockery which is amongst the best weapons of the Dutchman—especially the Amsterdammer.

The Dutch people had, indeed, every reason to be proud of their institutions and every reason to be attached to a way of life in which social planning and individual liberty were unusually well combined. Industrially, Holland had recovered a position as one of the most progressive of European states. Her traditional industries—agriculture, fishing and shipping—had been modernised and expanded. To these had been added new ones—radio, aircraft, textile, metallurgical, engineering and shipbuilding industries. Industrial research was well endowed and developed, and Dutch designers seem to have inherited all the ingenuity as well as the taste of their ancestors. Architects like Berlage and de Bazel succeeded in combining new ideas and materials with the best of the old traditions : nowhere in Europe are the old and the new more successfully blended than in the architecture of Amsterdam. Wages and standards of living were generally high, and the educational system and the medical services bore comparison with the best. In many of these fields, Britain might with advantage study Dutch methods. For his part, the Dutchman, cosmopolitan by tradition and multilingual by education, did not hesitate to go abroad to satisfy his wants, and in particular, to look to Britain for much of his reading. Shaw, Priestley, Huxley, D. H. Lawrence, Dorothy Sayers, even P. G. Wodehouse, and many others, were best-sellers in

Holland. The traffic was not entirely one-way. Lately, there has been a revival of imaginative fiction in Holland, and a few of the best novels—notably Arthur van Schendel's *The Johanna Maria* with a warmly appreciative preface by 'Q'—have been successfully translated into English. Musically, there was much less contact : since the early seventeenth century, when Sweelinck exchanged ideas with his English friends and contemporaries, John Bull and Peter Philips, Dutch music has been caught up in the German orbit. One or two of the younger Dutch composers—notably Willem Pijper—have become known in England. But Dutch musical opinion had been shaped by Mengelberg in the Brahmsian mould ; Mahler and Bruckner were its staple "modern" diet. Elgar, Delius, Vaughan Williams, Walton and Bliss were names which meant no more to Dutch music lovers than Diepenbrock or Vermeulen meant to us. (Sibelius, it may be added, was hardly better known.) Whatever may be the case with modern music, one cannot help feeling that, if opportunities for performance were given, the English Church music and madrigals of the sixteenth century and the choral and string music of Purcell and Locke and their contemporaries might well find favour with a musical public which for too long has been apt to accept the view that England is a 'Land ohne Musik.'

THE HARBOUR OF ROTTERDAM
Water colour by Mrs. Charles Toorop

In colonial affairs, Holland was in some respects ahead of Britain. The Englishman in Holland could hardly fail to be impressed by the widespread interest in colonial affairs and the knowledge of the problems of the colonial Empire. The Colonial Institutes and the emphasis on colonial affairs in the educational system succeeded in making the average Dutchman singularly well-informed as to the economic importance of colonies and in stimulating interest in careers in the overseas empire. An Englishman might well feel aware of his ignorance of his own Empire —a feeling not removed by the reflection that he shared this ignorance with large numbers of his fellow-countrymen. In Netherlands India great changes have come over the administration since the economic crisis of 1900. After a slow start, the Dutch Colonial administration has become one of the most progressive and efficient in the world. The old worship of spice and indigo has long since disappeared and the administration now supervises a vast range of agricultural and mineral production. The Dutch man—and Dutch woman—who went to the Colonies identified himself thoroughly with his surroundings: many were there to stay. So side by side with material progress has gone reform of the systems of education and native welfare. As J. S. Furnivall—himself a man of many years experience of administration in Burma—wrote lately on Netherlands India: "Burma might learn much from studying its neighbours . . . we might learn much where the Dutch may seem to have succeeded, and no less perhaps where it may seem that they have failed." There is every reason to hope that Japanese occupation will only prove a temporary setback, to be followed by strengthened Anglo-Dutch colonial collaboration.

What kind of a country may the English visitor to Holland after the war expect to find? If he has read his guide books, he will remember that their favourite adjective in describing Holland is "quaint." "Quaint," the dictionary tells us, means "daintily odd." Now any people less dainty or less odd than the Dutch it would be difficult to find. The Dutchman is essentially a forthright, frank and normal being—normal, some may think, to the point of dullness, for he has scant patience with eccentricity of any kind. It is one of the paradoxes of Holland that though essentially a highly-urbanised, cosmopolitan country where foreign influences are quickly appreciated and absorbed, the individual Dutchman, even the city dweller, retains a countryman's curiosity, embarrassing sometimes to a foreigner, about anything out of the ordinary in the way of clothes or customs: a pair of English flannel trousers and sports jacket was enough to cause a sensation in the Kalverstraat (Amsterdam's Oxford Street). It is only fair to add that the Dutch are equally capable of good-humouredly barracking a Volendammer up from the country for a Saturday night and wearing the Dutch national costume.

What is true of the people is just as true of the Dutch landscape, largely the work of generations of Dutchmen with their picks and shovels.

LEYDEN
Etching by Muirhead Bone

It was not a mere whimsy fancy which dotted Holland with windmills and gabled houses and intersected it with a thousand waterways. Pure practical necessity was the reason. The canals and the barges are the Dutchman's transport. The long narrow town houses with their brief facades were designed to make the best use of space in a country where the population was dense and land precious. The high-backed roof was the best way of dealing with a heavy rainfall. Utility has always been the watchword of a frugal and thrifty people; but we must not go too far; useful a thing must be, but ugly—never. If paint must be used to preserve, it can be bright and gay. If we must have a steep roof, let us give it a pleasing facade. If we have no stone, let us be sure that our bricks are mellow in colour and of the best dimensions. If our ground is soggy so that we must wear clogs, let us give them an attractive shape. Thus (I think) the Dutchman's thoughts ran. Carried to its highest point, it was a kind of perception which flowered into Dutch art. As 'Q' once wrote, ". . . in homely realism, lovingly studied and perfected for its own sake, Dutch art has always found its natural expression."

The Englishman will find himself, then, amongst a people who put practical values and achievements very high; a self-reliant, thorough-going and intelligent people who say what they think without fear or favour, know what they want and usually get it. He will not, if he is wise,

125

expect to be overwhelmed immediately with that effusive (and specious) hospitality to complete strangers in which the Germans specialised. He may miss the diplomatic restraint of English society which tolerates the fool perhaps too gladly. He may even feel that he is on probation until he is better known. His cherished opinions will be questioned by people who equally expect him to question theirs. In foreign and colonial affairs, he will find the Dutchman a realist but not a cynic. In domestic affairs, he will find that the ancient traditions of local freedom and local government still flourish. That freedom, though it retains a certain oligarchical character and is limited by a curious formal snobbery which has never quite disappeared, is based on a deeply-rooted individualism. And though individualism never quite degenerated into confusion, it came perilously near it—in the continual splintering process which divided the democratic parties and Protestant Churches (Holland is roughly half Catholic and half Protestant) into ever smaller units. There seems to be no doubt that the terrible years of occupation have arrested that process and restored a great measure of unity and strength to both democracy and Protestantism.

He will also find—what goes with individualism in Britain and America —a passion for sport, especially for football, hockey and rowing. This is the latest manifestation of the traditional Dutch affection for clubs, a tradition that goes back to the medieval gilds and schools of rhetoric and may be traced through the club mania of the eighteenth century down to the cycling clubs, Boy Scouts and religious organisations of the present day. The Dutch have their own versions of the University Boat Race and the Cup Final, uproarious national festivals where an Englishman could feel thoroughly at home. But the real unit of Dutch life as of English remains the home and the family.

The Dutch and the British have many things in common—the same love of personal and national liberty, the same respect for tradition, for precedent and for continuity, the same strong sense of political responsibility ; these qualities have enabled both peoples to overcome economic crises, to combine government and municipal planning with individual enterprise, and to prevent democratic institutions from sliding into chaos under the pressure of extremist agitation. For three centuries, these two peoples were seafarers, traders and manufacturers while elsewhere in Europe debased and corrupted forms of feudal tyranny were tottering towards collapse and revolution: and while trade has undoubtedly brought rivalry, it has also brought certain common interests and sympathies. With the passage of time, the rivalries have softened, and even colonies, the ancient bone of contention, tend nowadays to create common interests rather than obstacles to Anglo-Dutch co-operation. But none of these affinities, historical, economic or temperamental, is likely to be strong enough to lead to solid or permanent co-operation. The sovereign independence of a nation is, it seems, a treasure that is only likely to be parted

SOWING GRAIN
Drawing by Vincent van Gogh, 1881

with when the national existence is itself threatened. And here the threats of war may produce the incentive which the security of peace has failed to provide. The German attack upon neutral Holland in 1940 shattered the hopes of those who imagined that strict neutrality might offer a sure shield against aggression. Britain too has learnt bitter lessons. The nightmare of our rulers for centuries has been the possession of the Dutch and Belgian coasts by an enemy. In 1940, in a matter of days, nightmare became grim reality and to the hazards of the war at sea was added the bombardment of the cities of Britain from the airfields of the Low Countries. Finally, we have seen the emergence of long-range bombarding weapons which might well in a future war eliminate the ocean barrier which as late as 1940 was Britain's best defence. Now more than ever before the fate of Britain is inseparably bound up with that of the nations on the Western European seaboard : only common action can save Western Europe from its own ever-increasing capacity for destruction. There could be no better beginning than between these two nations which have borrowed and lent so long and so freely and which in this war stood together in loyal alliance through more than four long, dark years.